I0181425

An Incurable Disease:

Memories, Observations and Ravings from a Baby Boomer Cub Fan

An Incurable Disease

Memories, Observations and Ravings from a Baby Boomer Cub Fan

Frank Mucci

Copyright © 2013 by Frank Mucci

All rights reserved. No part of this book may be used or reproduced in any manner whatsoever without written permission, except in the case of brief quotations embodied in critical articles or reviews.

Published 2013 by HumorOutcasts Press
Printed in the United States of America

ISBN 0-615-87512-2
EAN-13 978-061587512-5

To my wife Jo, who, though only mildly amused by my writing, encouraged me through many periods of self-doubt and frustration so that I could complete a manuscript that in the end will probably bring little more than an occasional smile to her beautiful face.

Table of Contents

Introduction

*W*riting a book is a long, slow process. There's a lot involved in getting it just right. It's not something you jump into and expect to happen overnight. You take your time. You plan it out. You make sure you have all the pieces in place. And even then, when you think you have it just right, you begin to have doubts and find yourself rewriting and editing and copying and pasting until you think maybe, finally you have it.

It has taken me a few years to put this book together. Lots of writing, rewriting, editing, uncontrollable sobbing, drinking, rehabbing, re-drinking, re-rehabbing, self-doubt, and just plain giving up have made the process even slower and longer than it should have been. But at last I am calling this adventure, if not good, at least finished. The long, slow process has mercifully come to an end.

Building a championship team is also a long, slow process— apparently a hell of a lot longer and slower than that of writing a book, because, holy crap, you'd think after more than a century of long, slow processing, the Chicago Cubs would not only have a championship team, but it would be a team so great it could crush even the 1927 New York Yankees! But no, not even one hundred years of fermentation has been enough time for my Cubbies to become a world champion.

For baby boomers like me who have loved the Cubs since childhood, half of that century-long slump has unfolded right in front of our unbelieving eyes. Unbelieving because we all were naively certain that, unlike our folks, one day we'd get to see the Cubs win it all. Now, as we head into those wonderful "golden years" (Social Security, Medicare, afternoon naps, Depends, and Viagra), we're not so sure anymore. In fact, just *getting* to the World Series, let alone winning the damn thing, seems unlikely.

We've come close, sort of. Close to the World Series anyway— within a handful of outs. Twice! So close that we were silly enough to think it was finally gonna happen. Twice! But it didn't. Not even once. And so the droughts continue. Sixty-seven years since a World Series appearance and a-century-plus-four years since a world championship.

How is that even possible? *Is* that even possible? I wouldn't think so if I hadn't witnessed a large chunk of it myself.

And from that comes perhaps the biggest question: Why? Why do I keep witnessing this marathon? I'm smarter than that, right? But I keep on watching. I keep on loving those losers. I keep insisting, "NO MORE!" and then, unable to resist the hold they have on me, I come back for more.

It has gotten so bad that I've had to seek help. In fact the other day I was watching the Cubs and feeling sorry for myself and drinking myself into oblivion—pretty much what I do every day—when I started crying uncontrollably. Deeply concerned, my wife immediately called my psychotherapist—he's on speed dial—and scheduled another session for me. Following is a transcript from that session.

Psychotherapist: *So what brings you here today, Frank?*

Me: *I have some questions, Doc. Why do the stupid Cubs lose so much? I mean there has to be a reason, doesn't there? Why has it been so long since the Cubs have won a pennant or a World Series? You'd think they would even accidentally win a fucking championship sometime, wouldn't you? I bet over the course of a hundred years, even a team made up of one-legged nuns, blind midgets, and female impersonators would have accidentally won a fucking championship! Do you have the answer to any of these questions, Doc? Please, help me! You gotta help me!*

Psychotherapist: *I'm just a doctor, not a miracle worker. That'll be two-hundred dollars.*

As you can see, there is no cure for what I have, but I've discovered ways to deal with it and first and foremost living as a Cub fan requires the ability to laugh it off—to look at the absurdity of it all and somehow enjoy it. Sure I get mad and frustrated and disgusted at how bad the Cubs (and our luck) have been through the half-century I have loved them, but I also cherish every bit of their history—as awful as much of it is. And you have to admit it Cub fans, once you accept the fact that you've spent your life rooting for a team that is synonymous with losing and you peal away all the layers of disappointment and frustration, there's some pretty funny shit in there.

Enjoy the shit.

Part One: Getting to First Base

So You Wanna Be a Cub Fan, Huh?

Are you sure about that? If so, you've come to the right place because nobody knows more about what it takes to be a Cub fan than yours truly. Here you will find out how I became infected with this disease, discover why, despite all the losing, it is fun to be a Cub fan, and most importantly receive a list of rules that will help you get through the entire experience (memorize them at once!). Plus we'll talk about curses and myths, and take a look at some numbers that will surely test your resolve to become a fan of a team that will annually test your resolve to remain a fan.

Chapter 1: An Incurable Disease

I really didn't have a choice—I was born to be a Cub fan. When you grow up in a family of Cub fans, you really have no choice. You can also be born with good sense, but it doesn't matter. The Cubs will still steal your heart, your mind, and your soul and you will spend the rest of your life with an incurable disease.

I fell in love with the Cubs at age ten when I was too young and dumb to know any better—like the fact that girls have some nice bumps and curves and fun stuff under their clothes. Had I known then what I know now, I'd have skipped the stupid Cubs and gone directly to the girls.

I had already been acquainted with the object of my affection for several years, but it wasn't until the 1964 season that I fell head-over-heels, completely unaware that for the next five decades, the bumbling Cubs would annually do that exact same thing. I would run home from school to catch the last inning or two of my heroes on TV. By the time I got home, they'd usually be losing, but I really didn't care that much—not yet anyway. I thought that in time, the Cubs would be good and win lots of games. Hell, I was only ten—I had plenty of years ahead of me and the Cubs were bound to get better before I got old. And thus were the first signs that I was infected with an incurable disease.

Just so they could suck me in further before stomping all over me, the Cubs started winning games—not a lot of winning, but enough to mess with the mind of an easily persuaded and naïve kid. I had only been a fan a few years and already they looked to be on the verge of building a championship ball club. Of course that all fell apart and so did my dreams, but I was still just a teen and I had many Cubs seasons ahead of me. Idiot that I was, I thought they were bound to win it all sooner or later.

After more than a decade of unbelievably hideous crap passing for "baseball," the Cubs were good again and in 1984 came to within one win of going to the World Series. I believed it would happen. I was stupid. The Cubs never won that one game and I was starting to get frustrated. I was thirty—not getting any younger—and beginning to wonder if twenty years prior, I had maybe made a poor decision.

The Cubs floundered again with just a handful of decent seasons, but overall they sucked until 2003. That year, everything was falling into place and my Cubbies were on their way to finally getting to the World Series. I paced nervously counting down the outs—just five to go! Forgetting all the Cubs had taught me over the years, I started to believe again.

Yes, I had forgotten one of the primary rules for being a Cub fan: If you wish to maintain your sanity, never, ever expect victory. Ever! Hey, I'm talking to you stupid!

Then, Steve Bartman happened and after that everything changed. Sure, it was only a foul ball. Sure, the Cubs still had a 3-0 lead. Sure, they still only needed five outs. But just like any baby boomer Cub fan who had been through years and years of baseball hell, I knew what would happen next. I knew it! We all did. I'd tell you exactly what happened, but I'd probably puke all over my keyboard while writing the hideous details.

But I've learned to live with this disease. I no longer get so upset. I don't throw things at my TV. I don't get up and pace back and forth during tense moments. I just sit back in my recliner with a beer in one hand and the remote in the other. The Cubs leave the bases loaded for the umpteenth time. "Screw 'em," I mutter as I change to the Food Channel.

Even when the Cubs are playing well, I don't get as excited about it as I used to. In 2008, the Cubs won 97 games to lead the National League and headed to the post-season as favorites to play in the World Series. But I'm not a complete idiot. I have learned not to trust the Cubs and I was sure they'd fall on their collective asses. And when they did, I wasn't even that disappointed. I had a half-century of personal experience to know how it would all play out, so I was prepared. I drank a few beers and shook my head, "Same old Cubs."

Now when I go to Wrigley Field, I don't worry about the outcome of the game. I just sit in the bleachers, have a brew or two, people watch (plenty of fine looking women can be found in the Wrigley Field bleachers), and just look around the most historic stadium in baseball.

I look to my left at the center field bleachers and realize this is the area Babe Ruth's fabled "called shot" landed against the Cubs in the 1932 World Series. I look to my right toward the Cubs bullpen and see the spot where Bartman was sitting when he got his dirty, little hands in the way of what would have put the Cubs just four outs away from the 2003 World Series. I glance up at the big scoreboard to check the score just in case the Cubs have done something positive while I've been sitting here daydreaming. Nope, they're still losing to the horseshit Pirates, of all teams. Down on the field in front of me is the Cubs leftfielder, Alfonso Soriano, looking up to us in the bleachers as we hold up our fingers to remind him of how many outs there are in the inning. "What a dumbass," I say to my wife.

Sure, I want the Cubs to win, but I've learned not to get so upset if they lose. Like Jack Nicholson after receiving several shock treatments in *One Flew Over the Cuckoo's Nest*, I'm comfortably numb. It doesn't matter so much anymore. There's a good chance the Cubs will never win it all in my lifetime—I know this and I'm OK with it.

Of course, part of my duty as a Cub fan has been to pass this incurable disease on to the next generation. So my kids are Cub fans now, and some day they too will pass it on to their kids because that's their job. And they blame me for it too. My son asks me why I had to make him a fan of a team that never wins. I tell him he was born to be a Cub fan. On opening day 1977, my wife and I stopped at the doctor's office on our way to Wrigley Field to get official word that she was pregnant with our son. That day, though he was just a tiny fetus, he attended his first Cubs game and immediately got a taste of what his future would bring. The Cubs lost.

Because when you grow up in a family of Cub fans, you really have no choice. You can also be born with good sense, but it doesn't matter. The Cubs will still steal your heart, your mind, and your soul and you will spend the rest of your life with an incurable disease.

Chapter 2: Why Would Anybody In Their Right Mind Be a Cub Fan?

I may be stupid—and I probably are—but I take pride in being a Cub fan. I enjoy wearing my Cubs hat when I am out and about and I like wearing my Cubs t-shirts and Cubs jerseys and I like flying the Cubs flag I have hanging from my house. And I absolutely love getting drunk and running through the streets dressed in nothing but my Cubbie-blue jockstrap.

The point is, I don't think of being a Cub fan as the awful, painful experience that non-Cub fans seem to think it must be. I mean it does hurt, but somehow it's also fun. Call me a masochist.

Anyone reading this who is not a Cub fan may be wondering...

Why the hell am I reading this stupid crap?

But another thing he or she may be wondering is...

Why would anybody in their right mind be a Cub fan? I mean are these people into pain or something?

I have to admit that there seems to be a lot of negative stuff that comes with being a Cub fan, what with the losing and all that crap. But there is a lot more to being a Cub fan than wins and losses. The Cubs have more fans than any other team in the National League and obviously that isn't due to winning.

First off, we are not in our right minds—nobody is. There is evidence everywhere that humans are pretty screwed up. Sure, drugs, alcohol, and religion have played a role, but for the most part, people are messed up naturally. So no, being a Cub fan has nothing to do with having, or not having, a sound mind. All people are nuts.

As far as being into pain, being a Cub fan is not as painful as it is fun. We choose to be Cub fans because it's fun, not because it's easy. I suppose it's easy to be loyal to something that is always successful. Take the Yankees. How difficult is it to be a Yankees fan? They've won what, like a million pennants or something like that, right? Boy that takes a lot of commitment. But how much fun can it be for Yankees fans when they win? Isn't it expected? Isn't anything less than a win a disappointment? The real question is: Why would anybody in their right mind be a Yankees fan? Where is the joy of winning when winning is expected? Winning is fun when it isn't necessarily expected, or in our case, when losing is expected.

Now, let's get to the scientific part of all of this. Each sports fan has three built-in gauges: expectation, frustration, and celebration. If the level of expectation is high, the level of frustration upon failure is also high, and obviously, the level of celebration is at zero. If the level of expectation is high, the level of frustration upon success is low, but the level of celebration upon success—because success was expected—is only moderate. On the other hand, if the level of expectation is low, the levels of frustration and celebration upon failure are also low. Finally, if the level of expectation is low, the level of frustration upon success will be at zero, but the level of celebration upon success will be sky high!

Below are some really cool-looking charts I stayed up all night designing to illustrate all this complicated shit for you (Fig. 1). Now if you are chart-challenged, you may want to just move on to the next paragraph where I explain what all this stuff means. If, on the other hand, you understand charts, you will probably figure out what I'm driving at by just looking at the charts, so you can skip the next paragraph and join up with us later. It's your call—I'm there for you either way.

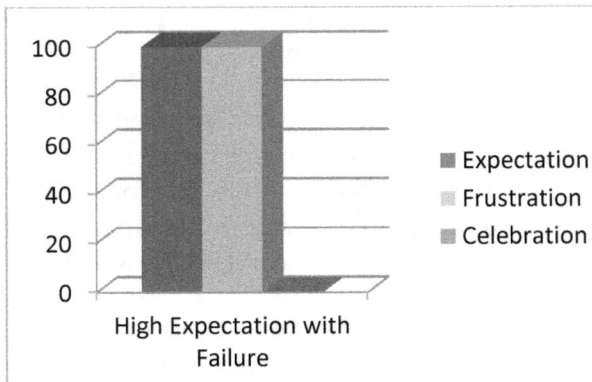

High Expectation with Failure

- Expectation
- Frustration
- Celebration

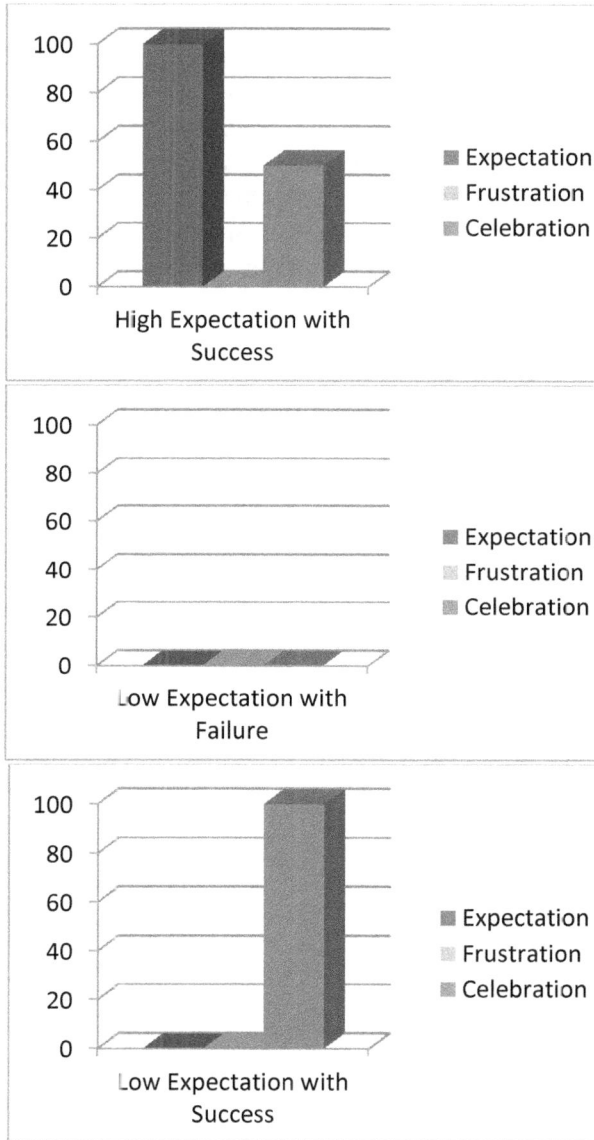

Fig. 1 – Really cool-looking charts I stayed up all night designing just to illustrate all this complicated shit for you

OK, if you are reading this paragraph, you must be chart-challenged. So what does all this mean? Two things: First, it means that I am pretty good at making charts. Secondly, it means Cub fans have more fun and are potentially happier people than Yankees fans. We have no expectations and therefore, we are rarely disappointed and frustrated. And on the rare occasion that we do win, the celebration is off the charts! Yankees fans, on the other hand, expect success and therefore are really bummed when they lose. And when they win, their attitude is like, "Another one? We won another one? Uh, OK, I guess we can find room on a shelf somewhere for another trophy. But, I'm not dusting the damn thing, OK? Someone else can dust it."

Hey, welcome back you brilliant chart person! We were just talking about how Cub fans are happier than Yankees fans, and... well you already know that because you are a chart wizard. Anyway, as I was saying, it is fun to be a Cub fan and so that is the answer to the question that is the title of this chapter: Why would anybody in their right mind be a Cub fan?

So next time some smartass asks you that question, just smack his Yankees cap off his fat, ugly head and yell, "Because it's fun!"

By the way, if he doesn't believe you, you have my permission to show him the charts.

Chapter 3: Simple Rules for Being a Cub Fan

*S*o you say you wanna be Cub fan, huh? Well, there are rules for being a Cub fan, and if you want to be a healthy, happy fan, you can't just jump into it without a full understanding of these rules. They are essential for getting through what are likely to be years of dashed hopes, unfulfilled dreams, and lots of heavy drinking.

Rule #1: Hate the White Sox.

This first one should come pretty easily because White Sox fans are soooo friggin' jealous of the fact that the Cubs own the city of Chicago that they are miserable, insufferable people. You'd think winning a World Series a few years ago would have ended all that, but actually they're worse than ever.

Anyway, part of being a Cub fan is enjoying any misfortune suffered by the White Sox. The more painful it is for Sox fans, the better. This means never, ever pulling for the Sox to win. Great day for a Cub fan: Cubs win; White Sox lose. Ultimate day for a Cub fan: Cubs sweep double-header; White Sox lose double-header. Since inter-league play was instituted, ultra-ultimate day for a Cub fan: Cubs beat the White Sox.

By the way, you can't be both a Cub fan and a White Sox fan— you have to be one or the other. If you like both teams, we don't want you. Pick a damn team and go with it!

Rule #1.5: Special Amendment to Rule #1.

Since inter-league play was instituted, a special amendment had to be added to Rule #1. As Rule #1 states, Cub fans should never pull for the White Sox to win, however, on occasion the White Sox play a team in the Cubs' division.

So the amended rule includes the following clause:

It is permissible to hope that the team the White Sox are playing loses if that team is in the Cubs' division and is within five games (either way) of the Cubs in the standings. Technically, this is not hoping the White Sox win, but rather hoping the other team loses.

Rule #2: Hate the Cardinals.

It's easy. Just hate them the same way you hate the White Sox.

Rule #3: Never expect victory.

If you wish to maintain your sanity, following this rule is essential. As a young, naïve Cub fan, I broke this rule many times, but quickly learned how painful that can be. It's kind of like sticking your hand in fire—the first few times, the flames are so beautiful that you can't help yourself, but eventually you catch on.

Of course, in spite of knowing all this, I broke the rule on October 14, 2003. My hands are still burning and I promise never to do that again.

Rule #4: Revel in victory.

While Cub fans should never expect victory, whenever it does happen you must enjoy it to the fullest. After the Cubs win, celebrate! High-five other Cub fans and yell "Cubbies!" Have several beers and enjoy the fact that you are drinking in celebration of success and not for the purpose of erasing unhappy memories of another blown save.

If you have friends that are White Sox fans, call the poor bastards and rub it in. (You may also want to reconsider your standards for selecting friends.) This is especially fun if the Sox also lose that day, but even if they win it'll still be fun because Sox fans are generally miserable people.

Rule #5: Pretend losing doesn't bother you.

This one just comes with experience—it'll get easier as time goes by. Sometimes, what I do is just pretend they didn't play. If the Cubs lose, I don't watch ESPN, I don't listen to sports radio, and I don't read the paper in the morning—it just didn't happen. In fact in 1997, the Cubs didn't start their season (at least in my mind) until two weeks after the season actually began.

Denial, denial, denial! It works... really it does.

Rule #6: It is OK to make fun of the Cubs, but never let outsiders do it.

If you are going to be a Cub fan, you must be able to maintain a sense of humor. You will experience horrible moments that would shatter the psyche of lesser humans, and the best way to counter those moments is through self-deprecation. Outsiders will have a hard time bashing your team if you beat them to it. But if someone does, don't let him get away with it—especially if he is a White Sox or Cardinals fan.

In those cases, it is totally permissible to suspend your good humor in favor of punching the bastard in the mouth.

Rule #7: Never, ever, under any circumstances do the wave.

Is there anything more annoying than the wave? Aside from the Kardashians, I mean.

Rule #8: Don't leave games early.

Cub fans stay until the final pitch... no matter how painful that may be.

Rule #8.5: Special Amendment to Rule #8.

I had to amend this rule too after I left a game early. It was in April of 2002 and we were sitting in the upper deck at Wrigley Field on the first base side. The temperature was about 35 degrees with wind gusts blowing straight at us from the North at around 40 miles per hour, and I called my wife and asked her to bring firewood. I have never been so cold in my life. The Cubs were losing something like 6-0 and it was the fifth inning, and they hadn't gotten the ball out of the infield, and we really couldn't feel our extremities.

So we went to Hooters and watched the NFL draft on TV. Was a hell of a good day!

Thus, the amended rule includes the following clause:

You are permitted to leave a game early if—and only if—frostbite is a very real possibility (Note: this may require a note from WGN meteorologist Tom Skilling).

Rule #9: It is OK to hate Ronnie "Woo Woo."

Sure Ronnie "Woo Woo" Wickers is a Cub fan, and that whole "Cubs Woo, Woody Woo" thing is kind of cute... for the first few seconds. But then it starts to really get on your nerves to the point that you want to **GRAB HIM AROUND THE NECK AND STRANGLE HIS SKINNY ASS!**

Of course you would never do that, but you have to admit, the thought does kind of bring a smile to your face, doesn't it?

Special Bonus Rule: If you have one of those little Cubs flags attached to your car window, never roll down the window while the car is in motion because you'll never see the damn thing again!

This one just seems like good common sense, don't you think?

*[Author's Note: This **never** happened to me.]*

Chapter 4: Curses, I Say!

*A*re the Cubs cursed?

For years, whenever there was talk about baseball curses, the two teams that always came up in conversation were the Boston Red Sox and the Cubs. Invariably, comparisons were made between the agonizing histories of the two franchises. Both teams were said to be cursed: "The Curse of the Billy Goat" (Cubs), "The Curse of the Bambino" (Red Sox). Infamous names were brought up: Lou Brock and Steve Bartman (Cubs), Bucky Dent and Bill Buckner (Red Sox). And then there were those damn years: 1908 (last Cubs championship), 1918 (last Red Sox championship), and 1945 (last Cubs World Series). It had reached a point where fans of both teams were happy to claim ownership of the label, "Most Abused."

But now that the Red Sox have finally won a couple World Series, we Cub fans can officially call ourselves the most cursed fans on the planet.

Of course, before the BoSox won all the marbles in 2004 and again in '07, their fans thought they wrote the book on suffering. To them I say, "Hah!" (Sorry, I spit a little bit.) I have nothing against the Red Sox or their fans. In fact I was happy when they beat the Cardinals in the '04 World Series—heck, I'm thrilled anytime the Cardinals lose. Before finally getting the monkey off their collective backs, however, the Red Sox had been to three World Series in my lifetime. Sure, they lost all three in seven games—that's got to be heartbreaking, I guess, but I wouldn't really know, because, **_THE CUBS HAVE NEVER PLAYED IN A WORLD SERIES IN MY LIFETIME!_**

Hell, The Curse of the Bambino wasn't even a curse. It was nothing more than an extremely poor front-office decision—worse than the Lou Brock trade. But nobody actually put a curse on the Red Sox. The Curse of the Billy Goat is the real deal, baby—at least in the sense that a curse was actually put on the Cubs. During the 1945 World Series, tavern owner William Sianis put a curse on the Cubs because they wouldn't let him bring his billy goat into the ballpark to watch the game. It seems Cubs management had some silly rule against bringing farm animals to the ballpark (if the White Sox had that rule it would cut their attendance in half). Sianis angrily declared that the Cubs would never again play in another World Series in Wrigley Field. And apparently the shelf life of a curse is much longer than that of he who casts it, because Sianis and the billy goat are dead, but the curse—real or not—lives on.

Not that I believe in that billy goat crap. I don't believe in the supernatural, I'm not at all superstitious, and I don't believe in curses, but we are now at sixty-seven years (and counting) since our last World Series. That, my friends, is a curse! Not a curse in the voodoo sense, but rather a curse in the "holy crap, I can't believe I've spent my entire life pulling for a team that never, ever catches a break" sense.

If you want to know what it is to really be cursed, just consider that the Yankees have Jeffrey Maier and we have Steve Bartman. Maier was a 12-year-old Yankees fan and Bartman was a 26-year-old Cub fan. Both interfered with a ball that could have been caught in the field of play. The difference? Maier reached over the wall in game one of the 1996 American League Championship Series to grab a ball hit by the Yankees' Derek Jeter and it was ruled a home run instead of fan interference. And, of course, the Yankees went on to win the game, the series, the pennant, and the World Series. Bartman reached over the wall in game six of the 2003 National League Championship Series to try to catch a foul ball hit by a Florida Marlin—it would have been the second out of the eighth inning. Instead it's just a foul ball, the Marlins rally, and the Cubs lose the game and the series. See the difference? The Yankees benefit from a pain-in-the-ass fan, and the Cubs get screwed by one.

Call it a curse or call it just plain bad luck. Either way it sucks.

Chapter 5: Go Figure

I like statistics. I like beer too. In fact I love beer, but aside from the fact that lots of people drink it at ballgames, and it is advertised on signs all over the ballpark, and every other commercial during ballgames has something to do with beer, beer really has little to do with baseball.

Statistics, on the other hand, have everything to do with baseball. In fact, statistics were invented shortly after baseball was invented because they needed something to put in the box scores. So I decided to take my fondness for numbers and do a statistical analysis of the Cubs. Originally, I was going to do a statistical analysis of my second favorite sport—nude coed beach volleyball—but it turns out they don't keep box scores.

Doing a statistical analysis of the Cubs was pretty easy because, unlike nude coed beach volleyball, baseball is the most statistically analyzed sport in the world and thanks to my good friends at Baseball-Reference.com, every statistic anyone could ever want about our national pastime is right there. Now I must warn you that this here chapter is going to be loaded with statistics. Some may be pretty, but most will be quite ugly because, after all, we are talking about the Cubs here.

So sit back and relax as I bring you...

A Statistical Analysis of Nude Coed Beach Volleyball

Oops... better make that...

A Statistical Analysis of the Cubs

It's true, the Cubs have been bad for a really long time, and a look at the numbers shows just how bad they have been. In more than one hundred years of World Series play, the Cubs have won ten National League pennants. That comes out to an average of about one World Series appearance every ten or eleven years. Sounds great, doesn't it? That would mean at least five World Series appearances in the roughly fifty years I have been following the Cubs. Unfortunately, all ten Cubs pennants came during the first forty-three years of World Series play. That comes out to an average of one World Series every 4.3 years for all those lucky dead Cub fans who were around during that period, and an average of 0.0 World Series appearances every sixty-six years since.

The Good

We'll start things off with the good numbers.

From 1903 (the year of the first World Series ever played) through 1945 (the year of the Cubs' last World Series), the Cubs' record is 3,675 wins and 2,867 losses, which is a very nice .562 winning percentage. Cub fans during those years had every right to expect victory, and an occasional World Series appearance from their team. They probably enjoyed being fans of a very successful team, but since they are all dead, we'll never know.

Unfortunately, we have to go way, way, way back to find really good New York Yankees-type numbers. From 1906 through 1910—a five-year period that includes an incredible 116-36 record in '06—the Cubs won four pennants and two World Series while posting 530 wins and only 235 losses. That's an amazing .693 winning percentage. That means they were winning seven out of every ten games. Unbelievable!

There were other good periods too, like the ten seasons that covered 1929 through 1938. The Cubs won four pennants during that period and compiled a record of 903-630, with a .589 winning percentage.

The Leo Durocher years were the best period for the Cubs during my lifetime. Over the six seasons that made up 1967 through 1972, the Cubs played .534 ball, winning 515 and losing 449. Of course there were no pennants during those years—just a couple of teases and some major heartbreak.

The Bad

Now we take a look at the crappy numbers.

From the years 1946 through 2011, the Cubbies have won 4,895 games and lost 5,523 games. That comes out to a .470 winning percentage—or more appropriately a .530 losing percentage. Now if this was like the 2000 presidential election, the Cubs might be named World Champions with a record like that, but in something as important as baseball, more always wins out over less.

During the fifty-two year period of 1960-2011 (the years I can remember so far), The Cubs have had just eighteen winning seasons, thirty-three losing seasons, and broke even just once. The Cubs' overall record during those years is 3,947 wins and 4,318 losses—a .478 winning percentage. In a way, I guess I shouldn't complain since that winning percentage is eight points higher than the .470 of the entire post-WWII era. So the Cubs have actually improved, if ever so slightly, over the years I've been a fan. But then my dancing has improved ever so slightly over the years too, and my wife will tell you just how good a dancer I am as soon as she's done laughing.

You say you want more, you crazy masochist? The Cubs have had some miserable stretches since their last World Series appearance. From 1947 through 1962—a period of sixteen seasons—the Cubs were able to post at least seventy wins in a season just four times. Included in that stretch were nine ninety-plus loss seasons. Their overall record during those years: 1,049 wins, 1,421 losses.

The years 1960 through 1962 were a particularly awful time to be a Cub fan. Our heroes had a record of 183-287 during that three-year black hole, which comes out to a putrid .3893 winning percentage.

It's a very close call if you want to talk about the worst back-to-back years because the Cubs had two sets of beauties. There were 1980 and '81, which brought a combined record of 102-163 and a .3894 winning percentage. Thankfully, the '81season was interrupted by a strike, otherwise, the Cubbies may have really stunk things up. But edging them out by a nose are the '61 and '62 teams when those two memorable years provided a combined 123-193 record and a .3892 winning percentage.

And then there is the wretched sound of 59-103 (.364 winning percentage). The Cubs did that in 1962 and enjoyed it so much they duplicated the feat four years later.

The Nauseating

And finally, that which makes me want to puke...

For a period of sixty years, 1901 (the beginning of baseball's modern era) through 1960, there were sixteen teams in the major leagues. Then in 1961, major league baseball expanded adding two new teams. The following year, two more were added, and the major leagues kept expanding periodically until the number of teams had nearly doubled to the present total of thirty.

In the fifty years of expansion, those of us who are baby boomer Cub fans have patiently waited for our team to make its first trip to the World Series in our lifetimes. During that time, twelve of the fourteen franchises that didn't even exist when we first became fans have played in a total of twenty World Series, winning nine of them. That works out roughly to one expansion team appearing in a World Series every four years while, during that same time, Cubs teams have appeared in a World Series every *NEVER* years.

That alone sucks, but seeing two franchises nobody gives a crap about—the Arizona Diamondbacks and the Florida (now Miami) Marlins (yuck!)—win it all in only their fourth and fifth years of existence respectively is just plain nauseating.

So there you have it—a lot of success early on and then years and years of a whole lot of poop. That's a crapload of numbers to digest and I'm sure you're as disgusted by some of them as I am. I thought of putting together some cool charts and fancy graphs and junk like that— you know, really do a big time statistical analysis—but then I got depressed by the numbers and started drinking and quite frankly, the charts probably would have looked like crap.

So that's enough statistics for one day. Now who's up for a few beers and a little nude coed beach volleyball?

Chapter 6: Swings and Mythses

I'm usually a very jovial guy—especially when I've been joviating—but there are a number of myths about the Cubs that have been floating around for years and it pisses me off! These myths have been repeated by ass clowns on sports talk radio and written about in newspaper columns for so long, they are now taken as the truth.

But now it's time to clear things up and I have taken it upon myself to cut through the crap and bring you the facts. So sit tight and read on. You may learn something.

Myth #1: Cub fans pack Wrigley Field just because it's Wrigley Field.

This ridiculous myth was born out of jealousy of White Sox fans and the stupidity of the media. True, Wrigley Field is a fabulous place to watch a ballgame, but Cub fans pack the stadium mainly because they love the Cubs. Much of being a Cub fan has to do with undying loyalty to the team and love for the entire Cub game experience—whether it is at home or away. Cub fans are baseball fans.

If the only reason Cub fans go to games is because of the ballpark, why are the Cubs the number one road draw in the National League? I don't have a rulebook handy, but I'm pretty sure that teams are not allowed to bring their home ballpark with them on the road. Wrigley Field stays in Chicago while the Cubs are out of town. Cub fans travel everywhere to see their team play—even to that piece of crap they call a ballpark on the South Side.

Sure Wrigley Field is great and the whole Wrigley experience is fun, but the main reason the Cubs outdraw the White Sox by a large margin is this simple fact: there are, and always have been, more Cub fans than Sox fans. A poll conducted by *Sports Illustrated* in 2004 indicated that 57 % of Illinois baseball fans are Cub fans. The White Sox finished a distant second at 13 % tied with the St. Louis Cardinals. That's right, there are as many Cardinals fans in the state of Illinois as there are White Sox fans!

Myth #2: White Sox fans are more knowledgeable and discriminating than Cub fans.

This one is an offshoot of Myth #1, where the idea is that the White Sox don't draw nearly as many fans as the Cubs because White Sox fans do not accept an inferior product. They are way too knowledgeable about baseball to be able to force themselves to sit and watch a game that is not being played properly—it's just too painful. Cub fans, on the other hand, are so stupid, and know so little about baseball, that they will go to any game on any day, even when the Cubs have a lousy team.

But if White Sox fans are so discriminating, doesn't it make sense that they would pack the ballpark when the team is playing well? These extremely knowledgeable fans would be really anxious to see the game played the way it's supposed to be played, right? In 2005, the White Sox won 99 games, finished in first place, and (get ready to puke, Cub fans) won the World Series, yet they drew only 2.3 million fans— ranking seventh of fourteen teams in the American League. So where were all those knowledgeable Sox fans? This has nothing to do with being knowledgeable or discriminating or anything like that. It has to do with having fewer fans and apparently a less appealing product.

Besides, if White Sox fans are so knowledgeable, why are they White Sox fans?

Myth #3: Cub fans don't care if the Cubs win or lose.

This myth is the bastard child of Myths #1 and #2. It goes something like this: We Cub fans only go to Wrigley Field because it's Wrigley Field, and we love to sit in the sun and drink beer, and we love the bars in the neighborhood, and it's just one big yuppie party. And we are baseball stupid. We really don't understand what those guys are doing running around in knickers with those thingies on their hands and trying to hit a little white ball with a stick. Therefore, we really don't care if the Cubs win or lose.

Here is the truth: Cub fans hate to lose! It drives us nuts and it eats at us every day. We get mad when our team plays lousy and we even boo them when they screw up—yes we boo. But we get over it, and we recover, and we are ready for more, because we love the Cubs and we love baseball.

Myth #4: White Sox fans hate the Cubs, but Cub fans don't hate the White Sox.

I have no idea where this one even got started because I've hated the White Sox all my life, so it's about time we got this cleared up once and for all. Now hear this: ***CUB FANS HATE THE WHITE SOX TOO!!!***

Sure, the first half of this myth is certainly true. White Sox fans are jealous and cranky about all the attention the Cubs get. Therefore, Sox fans are noisy and insufferable about their hatred for all things Cub. But, we Cub fans hate the White Sox too, we just don't think of that other team as being all that important in our lives. The White Sox are a nuisance more than anything else—like gnats buzzing around your face. Besides, we are too busy hating teams that actually matter—like the Cardinals. So yes, we are quieter about it, but believe me, good Cub fans delight in White Sox failure and futility. And we enjoy the fact that they hate us so!

Myth #5: Cub fans are far better looking than White Sox fans.

OK, this one happens to be true.

Part Two: Stealing Second

Ancient History

Part of being a Cub fan is having a clear sense of their long, storied past. In order to fully appreciate the awesome responsibility of being a modern, informed fan, you have to know about the good times (1908 and 1945) and the bad times (pretty much everything else) from Cubs history. After all, how can we knoweth wherefore we art if we do not knoweth from whence we cometh? Or some shit like that. Anyway, here's a quick history lesson featuring the Cubs' last championship team, their last World Series appearance, and the years we baby boomers will never forget (aside from the various black holes in our memories caused by excessive use of psychedelic drugs)—those crazy 1960s.

Chapter 7: Nineteen, Oh Wait: It's Merkle's Big Boner!

I hear you snickering out there. Yeah, I thought a boner was an erection too, but apparently it meant something different way back when. And when you talk about Chicago Cubs world's championships, you have to go to a time known as "way back when" because the last time the Cubs won a World Series, Jesus was only 1,908 years old. Yep, it's been 104 years since my Cubbies were champs and unfortunately I missed it by a mere forty-five years. Those who've experienced it tell me winning a World Series is a great thing, so it seems appropriate that we open this section with a little bit about that 1908 Cubs team.

Being the investigative kind of guy I am, I had fully intended to interview some of the players from that 1908 team just to get an idea of what it was like to play on a world champion, but in doing my research I discovered they're all dead. In fact if he were alive today, the youngest player on that team, "Kid" Durbin, would be 126 years old, and likely little more than sixty pounds of drooling beef jerky. So that whole idea went out the window.

Since 1908 was more than a century ago, I knew I would have to do some major research to learn about that championship season and being a super-duper geekazoid who fully embraces today's technology, I decided to "double-click the old mouse." After doing that, I took a nap, and then I hit the Internet. That's when I discovered a couple of pretty interesting things.

For instance, did you know that if you Google the words "naughty nurses" you get 956,000 hits? How cool is that?

The second thing I discovered was that in September of the 1908 season, the Cubs played a game against the New York Giants that ended in controversy due to a play history has dubbed "Merkle's boner." And if not for that play, the last Cubs world championship would have been in 1907, not 1908, adding yet another year to the miserable drought. So let us all give thanks, Cub fans, for Merkle and his big boner.

Merkle's Big Boner

It is September 23, 1908 and the Cubs and Giants are tied for first place with only a few games left in the season. The Polo Grounds, home of the Giants, is overflowing with rowdy and excited fans (Little known fact: New York's professional polo team played in a stadium called "The Baseball Grounds.").

[Author's note: Yeah, I made that up.]

The Giants' regular first baseman, Fred Tenney, has an ouchie of some sort, so manager John McGraw inserts seldom used 19-year-old Fred Merkle into the lineup. The game is tied 1-1 going into the bottom of the ninth inning when, with two outs and Moose McCormick on first base, Merkle singles, sending McCormick to third. The next batter hits an apparent game-winning single, McCormick crosses the plate and the Giants are now one full game ahead of the Cubs.

Oh, wait!

Bear with me as I thumb through the official baseball rulebook—give me a sec. Here it is...

John 3:16 states:

When a batted ball safely touches the ground in fair territory and there is a runner on first base, the runner must advance to second base. If he does not advance to second base, but instead chooses to run full speed to the clubhouse so he can be the first one in the shower, and a fielder touches second base while holding the ball, the dumbass is out. It is a force play, and if it is the third out, any runs that score on the play do not count and the dumbass who didn't touch second base is pulled from the shower naked and screaming and is executed by hanging. Furthermore, blah, blah, blah...

[Author's note: I'm way too lazy—and drunk—to look up the rule, so I just made it up. But the actual rule is probably pretty similar to the one I wrote—except maybe for the "blah, blah, blah" part.]

Now getting back to the play...

After the apparent game-winning hit scores McCormick from third, Merkle stops midway between first and second and takes off running for the Giants' clubhouse in centerfield. It's okay to do that from the bench, but if you're on base that can be a problem because of the rule I posted above (See John 3:16).

With fans all over the field and many of the players already showering and snapping towels at one another, Johnny Evers, the Cubs second baseman, having noticed that Merkle never touched second base, ends up with a ball, finds one of the umpires, tells him what's up, and touches the bag. The umpire rules Merkle out leading to a lot of arguing, and accusations, and finger pointing, and general ugliness.

The Giants angrily file a protest to the league president who eventually rules in favor of the Cubs, declares the game a tie, and announces that the game, should it have any bearing on the pennant race, be replayed in its entirety at the end of the season. Of course, the regular season indeed ends with the Cubs and Giants tied for first and, as you've probably guessed by now, the Cubs win the game behind the outstanding pitching of everyone's favorite digitally-impaired hurler, Mordecai "Three-Finger" Brown.

The Cubs go on to beat the crap out of the Detroit Tigers in the World Series and for the second straight year, THE CUBS ARE WORLD CHAMPIONS!!! I can't believe I just wrote those words.

And all because of Merkle's big boner.

Frank Mucci

- 32 -

Chapter 8: The Spoils of War

*A*s a man who has seen his favorite team turn what should be a reasonable request—*Play in a freakin' World Series before I die!*—into an apparent impossibility, it comes as no big surprise to me, or anyone else, I'm sure, that the Cubs' last trip to the World Series occurred during a period when children, old men, and amputees played in the major leagues.

It was 1945—the final year of THE BIG ONE: WORLD WAR II. Over the past four years, a large number of the game's greatest players had been called to arms and major league team owners were left scrambling to fill their depleted rosters with any warm bodies they could find.

With apparently no regard for child labor laws, The Cincinnati Reds called on 15-year-old Joe Nuxhall to pitch for them in 1944. Equipped with a permission slip from his mommy, Nuxhall made one appearance for the Reds and showed that he wasn't quite ready for primetime: one inning pitched, two hits, five walks, five runs, and a 45.00 ERA. After that disastrous performance, the youngster was given a Saturday detention and didn't return to the major leagues until the ripe old age of twenty-three.

And speaking of old men, in 1945, no less than twenty different players past the age of forty turned in their AARP cards and cancelled their afternoon naps for another chance to put on knickers and act like kids again. Included among the oldsters was 42-year-old Paul Schreiber of the New York Yankees whose last major league action had come more than two decades prior, shortly after World War I ended. The man apparently only worked when the country was at war.

Baseball teams were indeed desperate, and nowhere was that desperation more apparent than in the city of St. Louis where the Browns—already considered second class citizens to their cross-town rivals, the Cardinals—looked everywhere for help and ended up with an unknown, lifelong minor league outfielder on their roster by the name of Pete Gray. At age thirty, Gray was coming off a great year in the minors and seemed to have everything any team could want. Everything, that is, except a right arm.

Having two arms would seem to be one of the prerequisites for anyone seeking employment as a major league baseball player, what with the hitting, throwing, catching and all. But again, these were desperate times and a one-armed baseball player is desperation personified. Of the thousands of available men in possession of varying degrees of baseball talent—and presumably two arms—the Browns weighed their options and decided to go with Gray. Throughout the minor leagues were players hoping for a shot at the majors and yet they just weren't good enough to beat out a guy missing a seemingly important appendage.

Imagine the letters home from those who didn't make the cut.

Dear Mom & Dad,

Well it looks like another year in the minors for me. Got beat out by a guy with one amazing arm.

Gotta go now...

Hell, at least the kid didn't *really* lie to his parents.

But give Gray credit. He managed to bat .218, which by my math means he would have hit an incredible .436 with two arms!

Fortunately, none of the Cubs' key players were in the military during the '45 season. Star players Phil Cavarretta, Stan Hack, Bill Nicholson, and Andy Pafko were available all season long, but in St. Louis, the defending champion Cardinals had to try to get by without star outfielder Stan Musial who was off fighting in THE BIG ONE. Additionally, every member of the Cubs had all of his body parts, was old enough to shave, and was young enough to remember what he'd had for breakfast.

Taking advantage of the Cardinals' misfortune of losing Musial, the Cubs marched through the season and on September 29, clinched the National League pennant in Pittsburgh by taking the first game of a double-header with the Pirates. When the season ended, the Cubs' record was 98-56, three games ahead of the second place Cardinals.

Although there is no way of knowing for sure, it seems reasonable to say that a great hitter like Musial would mean at least three games to his team, and probably a lot more. So, the Cubs could certainly thank THE BIG ONE: WORLD WAR II for assisting in their 1945 pennant. Not that the Cubs should apologize for that—no one should *ever* apologize for winning—especially not the Cubs!

But not even the war could help the Cubs in the '45 World Series. Due to travel restrictions during the war, the first three games were played in Detroit and games four through seven were in Chicago. (Apparently it wasn't easy to travel all the way from Chicago to Detroit and back to Chicago while a war was going on in the Pacific.) So the Cubs, who I guess hitch-hiked there, opened the series in Detroit and won two out of three before returning to Chicago needing to play just .500 ball at home. But these were the Cubs and this was 1945 and an old man with a goat was waiting for them.

Anyway, the Cubs lost games four and five and nearly blew game six before winning it in the twelfth inning to send the series to a seventh and final game. But game seven was a disaster with the Tigers pounding the Cubs 9-3.

The series was over and Cub fans were sad, but their spirits were no doubt lifted when they realized that in forty-two years of World Series play, their team had already played in ten Fall Classics. At that rate, they'd only have to wait another four years or so before their heroes would be back in another one.

Hell, that ain't so bad...

Chapter 9: Flunking Out of College

*F*ollowing a 1960 season in which the Cubs finished with an ugly 60 win, 94 loss record, team owner Phil Wrigley—ever perceptive—could tell something wasn't quite right and he was going to do something about it. He had had enough.

You see, if you keep changing managers, as Wrigley had over the years, and you keep getting the same crappy results, then you start thinking maybe you're going about this whole thing the wrong way.

> *Maybe the problem is this whole manager thing. Every manager I hire ends up getting fired because under his leadership we suck. Maybe we shouldn't have a manager at all. Maybe we would do better without a manager. Yes, that's it! What we need is no manager.*

So Wrigley called a press conference to announce that he had come up with a revolutionary idea—one he believed would forever change the way baseball teams would be managed on the field. It couldn't miss! It was fantastic! How could he have not thought of it sooner?

Wrigley's idea was to replace the field manager with a "College of Coaches"—not just one guy anymore, but an entire group of brilliant baseball men who would rotate throughout the entire Cubs organization and take turns as "head coach" of the major league team. The head coach would, in essence, act as the field manager of the team, but the key here is he really wouldn't be a manager—he would actually be a head coach. OK? Got that? See the difference?

Each coach would have an opportunity to see the Cubs talent (I use the term loosely) at all levels of the organization, and therefore help speed the development of young players. To be fair, that part of the plan seems like a pretty good idea, but where is the logic of having the head coach (manager) be part of the rotation. Wouldn't you want some continuity in that particular area? But hey, after fourteen straight continuity-filled seasons without a winning record, who could argue?

Among the original members of the "College of Coaches" were such baseball legends as Elvin "El" Tappe, Golden "Goldie" Holt, Harold "Harry" Craft, Verlon "Rube" Walker, and Vedie "Vedie" Himsl. If you've never heard of any of these guys, don't feel bad—they're own wives barely knew who they were.

Now, I'm going to warn you, I did a whole lot of research and I will be throwing a big bunch of numbers at you and most of them will not be pretty. These numbers will give you an idea of just what a great plan this "College of Coaches" thing was.

1961

The new "College of Coaches" era got off to a somewhat rocky start under the leadership of Vedie Himsl—the first head coach in baseball history—who finished the year (and as it turned out, his career) with a 10-21 record. While ten wins may not sound like much, it is tied for the record for most wins ever by any guy who won ten games.

Harry Craft was in charge for just sixteen games, but did considerably better at 7-9, and El Tappe captured the most wins with 42 while losing 54. But Lou Klein was tops of the four Cubs head coaches in '61 with an almost .500 record of 5-6. Add all this crap together and you end up with a 64 and 90 record—an improvement of four wins over the previous year.

After one year, the experiment was working!

1962

If year one was a step in the right direction, year two was several giant leaps backwards. Tappe and Klein returned to captain the ship along with newcomer Charlie Metro. Craft had taken over as manager of the new Houston Colt .45s franchise (yes, Houston had some harebrained idea about having a manager instead of a head coach) and Himsl, apparently did not impress enough with his .323 winning percentage to be brought back for year two.

But my man Vedie ended up looking like Frank Chance after Tappe's showing during the '62 season. In twenty games, Tappe managed to inspire the Cubbies to a four and sixteen record. Klein was better, winning twelve of thirty games and Metro's record was 43-69. Throw all this slop together, and you end up with 59 wins and 103 losses.

Something was not right—time to try something new.

1963

And when a man like Phil Wrigley decides to try something new, he comes up with shit no one else would ever think of.

Just as people started to question the wisdom of a rotating coaching system, Wrigley came up with yet another one of his "Holy shit, what the hell's he doing?" ideas: an athletic director. The man he chose for the position was retired Air Force colonel Robert V. Whitlow because, as we all know, decorated World War II flyers make the best baseball athletic directors. If you don't believe that, just check the list of greatest baseball athletic directors of all time and Whitlow's name is at the top of the list... and at the bottom too, because he *is* the list.

Exactly what Whitlow's new position would entail was anyone's guess considering no team had ever had one before. To his credit Whitlow did bring in the revolutionary idea of weight training which until then had never been tried in baseball. But what the Cubs needed wasn't more muscle. What they needed was more talent. Unfortunately, the only thing Whitlow was particularly talented at was shooting down Nazi aircraft, which up to that point had never been considered an essential baseball tool.

With Whitlow athletically directing the Cubs, the team responded with their first finish above .500 in seventeen years compiling a record of 82 wins and 80 losses. That's right, the Cubs had a winning record! But Whitlow wasn't the only thing new in '63. For the first time since the college was introduced, the Cubs had just one head coach all season—Bob Kennedy.

At last, the "College of Coaches"—or should I say, "College of **Coach"**—was working!

1964

After the surprising success of the '63 campaign, Cub fans could not wait for the 1964 season to begin. We had this new "College of Coach" thing going and a Nazi-killing athletic director and we were coming off a winning record and everything was just looking rosy.

OK, so it didn't turn out to be the great year we had hoped for, but Kennedy did manage to lead the Cubs to an almost respectable 76-86 record. After the numerous sub-seventy win seasons the Cubs had had through the '50s and early '60s, this didn't look so bad. Besides, we had the winningest head coach in the history of baseball head coaches. Kennedy's two-year win total of 158 far exceeded runner-up Tappe's total of 46.

1965

The 1965 season saw the Cubs scrap the "College of Coach" idea and return to the "College of Coaches" thingy. After leading the Cubbies to a 24-32 record, Kennedy was replaced by Lou Klein, who returned from a two-year absence to join the rotation. The Cubs responded by going 48-58 under Klein's leadership to bring the season totals to 72 wins and 90 losses.

Epilogue

After five years of the great "College of Coaches" or "Coach" experiment, the Cubs' record was 353 wins, 449 losses (for the mathematically impaired, that is 96 games under .500), and a .440 winning percentage. Col. Whitlow, who recognized a badly damaged aircraft when he saw one, ejected from his seat as athletic director eventually landing safely as nothing more than a little known footnote* in the annals of baseball.

Once again, Phil Wrigley knew something just was not right and he was going to do something about it. You see, if you keep changing head coaches, as he had over the past five years, and you keep getting the same crappy results, then you start thinking maybe you're going about this whole thing the wrong way.

Maybe the problem is this silly College of Coaches thing. Every coach I put in there ends up getting rotated out because under his leadership we suck. Maybe we shouldn't have a "College of Coaches" at all. Maybe we would do better with... um... let me think... I've got it! A manager!

Here's an example of a little known footnote. It'll be our little secret.

Chapter 10: Where Have You Gone, Cuno Barragan?

*I*n the game of baseball, perhaps the most important player on the field is the catcher. Take away the catcher and any pitch not hit by the batter would either knock the umpire on his fat ass (not necessarily a bad thing) or go completely past everyone and all the way to the wall behind home plate. Any runners on base would easily advance as fielders scramble for the loose ball. It would take hours just to play one inning.

Luckily, the inventers of baseball figured that out early on and, after considering the options, made the stupidest guy they could find crouch down behind the plate. They originally called the position "the stupid guy crouched down behind the plate who catches the ball so we don't have to chase after it," but later shortened the name to "catcher." A few months and several dead catchers later, the facemask was invented. Chest protectors and shin guards soon followed and it wasn't long before baseball fans appreciated the importance of having a catcher.

Let's fast-forward one century to the 1960s. Catchers were still important, but apparently the Cubs hadn't gotten the memo because from 1960 through 1965 the Chicago National League ball club was without a catcher. Not literally—they found plenty of guys during that period stupid enough to crouch behind the plate—but figuratively. In fact one expert calls Cubs backstops of that six-year span "the worst collection of catchers I've ever seen. I mean really, they sucked! The Cubs might as well have not had a catcher at all."

That's a direct quote from noted baseball historian and celebrated author Frank Mucci, so you know it just *has* to be true.

But who were these men? And were they really that bad? You be the judge.

1960

If you were a catcher looking for a job in 1960, a good place to fill out an application was at 1060 West Addison Street in Chicago. The Cubs employed no less than eight catchers on a team that lost 94 games.

Number one on the list in games played that year was none other than Moe Thacker. One look at Moe's hitting numbers shows his strength must have been in his defensive skills because, holy crap, he was an awful hitter. Thacker batted .156 and offset that anemic batting average by pounding out a grand total of zero home runs.

Next in line in games caught was Elvin Tappe, who in '61 would become part of another collection of incompetents—the "College of Coaches." Apparently the hitting half of the Thacker/Tappe combination, he batted .233 while matching Moe's big home run total. As good as these two guys were, however, the Cubs had a secret weapon on the bench in "Slammin' Sammy" Taylor, who batted .207 and led all Cubs catchers with three—count 'em, *three!*—home runs. The fourth and final Cubs catcher to see any significant action was Earl Averill, whose .235 average showed he could almost, kind of, hit.

The other four catchers the Cubs employed that year played in fewer games than the big four, so just imagine how shitty they must have been!

1961

Despite the wild success of the eight-headed monster the previous year, the Cubs managed to make it through the '61 season using just four catchers and in so doing discovered that less is definitely more.

Rookie Dick Bertell did most of the catching apparently based on his bat and not his mitt. In 90 games behind the plate, he committed an amazing total of twenty-three passed balls, which, combined with seventeen wild pitches, means a lot of the time it didn't much matter whether or not he was there. He did, however, produce a .273 batting average. After what Cub fans had witnessed the previous season, Bertell must have looked like Gabby Hartnett.

Sammy Taylor provided some pop off the bench with eight home runs, while Thacker showed his previous year was no fluke by posting a .171 average. But, the best story of the year belonged to 29-year-old rookie Facundo "Cuno" Barragan who belted a home run in his first major league at bat! Cub fans had to be excited about the potential of their exciting new catcher.

1962

The '62 season saw Bertell's bat continue to keep him in the lineup—at least batting average-wise (.302)—but somehow he only managed to drive in eighteen runs which were just two more than his sixteen passed balls. As catchers go, Bertell would have made a good gate.

Once again, Thacker dazzled with his bat while raising his average—this time to .187. At this pace, Big Moe would likely break the .200 barrier by the end of the century. Thacker, showing great consistency, also handled the pressure of matching his home run totals from the previous two years by again smashing zero.

The promise of Barragan's first at bat home run the year before, earned him considerably more playing time. While Cuno couldn't duplicate his home run totals (1) of '61, he did manage to surpass the coveted .200 mark by one point, which no-doubt made Thacker wonder how secure his job would be. An old face from the eight-headed monster of 1960, El Tappe, returned in '62 to remind everyone what they had missed—Tappe batted .208. The end of the season also brought the end of the Sammy Taylor years, who could muster just a .133 average.

1963

Somehow, the Cubs managed to make it through the '63 season without Thacker's booming bat. He was traded to the Cardinals who apparently had never seen him play.

In 99 games behind the plate, Bertell began to look like he was catching on to this catching thing. His passed ball total dropped to ten, but his batting average dropped with it—all the way down to .233.

Apparently, Dick was not a multi-tasker. He could hit, or he could catch, but he couldn't do both at the same time.

Joining Bertell to handle the catching chores were a couple of new faces, Jimmie Schaffer and Merritt Ranew. Schaffer, who came over in the Thacker deal, put up numbers Moe could only dream of: .239 average, seven home runs. Ranew did the work behind the plate in just 37 games, but played in a total of 78 games mainly due to a bat that produced an *amazing* .338 average. That's right—.338!

Sadly, the Cuno Barragan era came to a disappointing end. Barragan, played in just one game, batted once, and struck out. As it turned out, Cuno's home run in his first career at bat was the only one he would ever hit. Thus ended a career that began with a BANG! and sputtered to a halt with the sound of *Whiff.*

1964

The relative success of the catching crew in '63 seemed to disappear over the winter and was replaced with the usual crap. Bertell continued to struggle with the bat, hitting just .238, and Schaffer, now firmly entrenched as the number two catcher started to hit like a guy firmly entrenched as the Cubs' number two catcher (.205).

Newcomer, Vic Roznovsky, came up from the minors and quickly showed that he fully understood what it meant to be a Cubs catcher. The tall redhead wasted little time making Cub fans nauseous with his .197 batting average. Meanwhile, Ranew's average dropped an incredible 247 points from the previous year all the way down to .091. That still stands as the record for the biggest drop in average by a guy who didn't die during the offseason.

1965

Apparently Cubs management had had enough of Dick Bertell and decided to give some of the other guys a chance. Most of the catching duties were split three ways between youngsters Roznovsky and Chris Krug, and veteran Ed Bailey. In Bailey, the Cubs had acquired a real, true-life major league hitter. It's too bad the last time Bailey had actually been a real, true-life major league hitter was back in the '50s. Now, Bailey was a real, true-life major league has-been.

Roznovsky improved on his rookie showing by hitting .221, and Krug, a tall rookie, kept the tradition of lousy-hitting Cub catchers alive by turning in a .201 average. One thing you have to say about Cub rookie catchers of that era: they couldn't hit.

Epilogue

After the season ended, Roznovsky and Krug were getting ready to do battle for the starting job in '66. Cub management, apparently not at all interested in seeing who would win the epic battle between these two, made a trade with the San Francisco Giants that brought an unknown minor league catcher by the name of Randy Hundley to Chicago.

Roznovsky and Krug were both sent packing and the job was handed to Hundley. He responded by belting 19 home runs his rookie year (more than the combined totals of any of the catching combos the Cubs used in any of the previous six years) while displaying outstanding defensive skills.

The Cubs had finally found a catcher who could multi-task!

Chapter 11: The Brock Trade This and the Brock Trade That

*I*f you are a Cub fan, you have probably heard about "the Brock trade." How could you not have heard about it? For nearly half a century sports writers have written about the Brock trade.

They write things like, "The Cubs are dummies because they traded Lou Brock." Or, "No wonder the Cubs never win anything. They traded Lou Brock... those dummies."

It's always the Brock trade this and the Brock trade that.

True, it turned out to be a bad trade for the Cubs, but come on, GET OVER IT! It was not the worst trade ever made—does The Curse of the Bambino ring a bell? And no one ever talks about how the Cubs made a great trade in getting Ryne Sandberg from the Phillies. I guess Sandberg didn't do a whole lot... except win an MVP award in '84, collect ten Gold Gloves, smash nearly 300 career home runs, and gain entry into the Hall of Fame.

But let's get back to the Brock trade because if you're gonna be a Cub fan, you have to know about the Brock trade. In 1964, Lou Brock was in his third season with the Cubs as their starting leftfielder and despite great potential, he just couldn't seem to put it all together. He could run like the wind but with only a .250 average, he didn't get on base enough to use it. He had a strong arm, but fans in the box seats on the first base side often had to duck when he uncorked wild throws. After two-and-a-half years, it was beginning to look like Brock would never become anything more than a pretty good player.

The Cubs of the early '60s had some hitting with stars Ernie Banks, Billy Williams, and Ron Santo. What the Cubs lacked was pitching—everyone knew it and everyone said it.

Sports writers would write things like, "The Cubs are dummies because they have no pitching." Or, "No wonder the Cubs never win anything. They have no pitching... those dummies."

It was always no pitching this and no pitching that.

So, the Cubs decided to do something about their pitching. The St. Louis Cardinals had some pitching—an abundance of pitching and one of their best was Ernie Broglio. In '64, Broglio was coming off an 18-8 season and had won twenty-one games in 1960. From '60 through '63 he had won sixty games. Pretty good numbers—don't you think? The Cubs thought so, and they also thought the 29-year-old right-hander was just the kind of pitcher they needed.

On June 15, the Cubs pulled the trigger on the trade that forever would become a part of their lore. The two teams shuffled a number of players back and forth in the deal, but the two guys anyone remembers were Brock and Broglio. The Cubs finally had the pitcher they wanted and all it cost them was a guy who would likely drive the Cardinals crazy with unfulfilled potential. "Good luck!" the Cubs chuckled.

But of course we all know what happened, don't we? It turned out that the Cardinals—conniving little weasels that they are—never told the Cubs that Broglio was damaged goods. It seems that Broglio's arm had actually fallen off earlier that season. Desperately, the Cardinals ran to the morgue and replaced Broglio's missing appendage with the arm of a corpse. I'm not making this up! The Cardinals had actually taken the arm of a corpse and stuck it on Broglio's right shoulder with some duct tape and then said, "Here you go Cubbies (snicker, snicker), here's one of our best pitchers. We hate to give him up, but we just have so darn many good pitchers that it's embarrassing. So here, take him (snicker, snicker). Consider it an early Christmas gift."

And so the Cubs had their man Broglio. He pitched the rest of the '64 season, plus two more years with the Cubs before calling it quits. His record as a Cub: 7 wins, 19 losses, 5.40 ERA. Sure, those are some terrible numbers, but all things considered—what with the fact that he was pitching with the arm of a corpse—he did pretty well.

Brock on the other hand was equipped with an entire array of his own body parts and the moment he put on a Cardinals uniform magically started using them to their full potential. He batted .348 the remainder of the season while leading the Cardinals to the World Series and ended his career with more than three thousand hits, the single-season and career records for stolen bases, and ultimately, induction into the Hall of Fame.

So that's the Brock trade. Those dirty, rotten Cardinals deceived the Cubs and gave them a broken-down pitcher, and for nearly fifty years, we Cub fans have had to deal with it. No matter whom the Cubs steal from other teams doesn't seem to matter—we still have to hear the same old crap about how the Brock trade is the worst trade ever.

So next time you see a Cardinals fan, just punch him in the mouth. It won't change anything, but you'll feel a lot better.

[Editor's note: We do not in any way condone acts of violence towards Cardinals fans. White Sox fans? Sure, but not Cardinals fans.]

Chapter 12: Going Camping With Leo

*A*fter the College of Coaches blimp had crashed and burned like the Hindenburg, Phil Wrigley, apparently fresh out of harebrained schemes, found himself with no choice but to get back into the market for the very thing he was sure just five years ago he didn't need—a major league manager.

The Cubs owner was never comfortable with convention having long resisted the lure of night baseball and blazing his own trail with an Air Force colonel athletically directing his manager-less ball club. If Wrigley could have figured out a way to field a team without players, he probably would have tried that too. But baseball is no place for new ideas—especially stupid ones—and so Wrigley decided if he was going to go back to that silly tradition of having one man lead his ball club, that man wasn't going to be just another guy he'd have to fire in a year or two. He wanted a manager with a resume that included the words "Won a World Series" under the "Major Accomplishments" line.

So Wrigley once again shocked the baseball world by hiring a man who at age sixty hadn't skippered a team in ten years. Despite his past successes, Leo Durocher's combative personality was considered an owner's nightmare, which apparently didn't bother Wrigley whose ball club had been a Cub fan's nightmare ever since the end of World War II. No wallflower, Durocher immediately made it clear that he was *not* brought in to be a head coach nor would he be part of a rotating college and there'd be none of that athletic director bullshit either. He was hired to manage the Cubs and he was going to do just that.

Leo took over a team featuring the superstar trio of Billy Williams, Ron Santo, and Ernie Banks. But surrounding that great nucleus was an abundance of crap, crap, and more crap. One of Durocher's first goals was to wean Cub fans off of the constant presence of "Mr. Cub." In Leo's eyes Banks, despite years of greatness, had two big strikes against him. At 35, Ernie's best years were way behind him and—perhaps worse—he was a nice guy. After all, Durocher was the man who had once famously declared "Nice guys finish last." But Banks was also a competitor and his manager's desire to send him out to pasture merely steeled his determination to stay in the lineup, which he did.

While Banks may have been a nice guy, Durocher definitely was not. Years of arguing with umpires, opponents, teammates, his players, and his bosses had earned Leo numerous suspensions and a reputation as being *anything* but nice. When Durocher's initial season as Cubs boss (1966) thudded to a merciful conclusion, it was evident that it's not only agreeable gentlemen who finish buried in the cellar, pricks do too. The Cubs' 103 losses earned them that spot and left Cub fans longing for Wrigley's old system so that Leo could be rotated right out of the dugout and out onto his ass. But Durocher didn't get where he was by being stupid and as Cub fans suffered through the misery of another season from hell, the crap, crap, and more crap that had customarily surrounded their trio of stars had been replaced by youngsters with actual talent.

The following year, that young talent began to develop and for the remainder of Durocher's reign as manager, the Cubs would be a pennant contender. But of Durocher's seven seasons as Cubs manager, the one that will forever define his stay in Chicago is 1969. That's the one baby boomer Cub fans have tattooed on our brains. The one that led us on the road to becoming the cynical fans we are today. Much has been written about that team and that season (including the next chapter), but perhaps most interesting about that year was Leo's sudden weekend disappearance.

It was Saturday, July 26, and the Dodgers were in town for a nationally televised game and the Cubs were securely in first place by five games over the Mets. Shortly after the game started, Leo told third base coach Pete Reiser that he wasn't feeling well, handed him the lineup card, and left the ballpark. That's not terribly unusual. Who among us hasn't had to go home early due to sickness? Only difference is, Leo didn't go home, nor did he go to the hospital. Instead he went to camp.

Earlier that season, Leo had married for the fourth time. This time the new Mrs. Durocher was Chicagoan Lynne Goldblatt whose son was spending the summer in Wisconsin at Camp Ojibwa. As any newly married man will tell you, when the little woman wants something, you give it to her because she may never give *it* to you again. And what Mrs. Durocher wanted was for the hubby to cross the Cheddar Curtain and join her for the weekend at her son's summer camp. Perhaps Mrs. D didn't understand that her husband's job wasn't one that included vacation time, but it didn't matter because Leo, fearing the wrath of his new bride more than that of his boss, feigned sickness, leaving his ball club in the hands of his coaching staff.

The Cubs split the two weekend games to remain solidly in first place and no one suspected a thing. It wasn't until later that Leo's camp trip was uncovered by reporters and after the Cubs collapsed in September, Durocher's lack of dedication to his team that weekend in July was cited by reporters—most of whom detested Leo—as one of the reasons why.

Did Leo's camp visit contribute to his team's monumental fall? Who knows and who cares? The real story here is that the hard-nosed, no nonsense, cantankerous Durocher—a symbol of total dedication to the game of baseball—was as pussy-whipped as the rest of us.

Chapter 13: Nineteen Six-Denial

Cub fans not old enough to remember 1969 see that the Cubs finished eight games out that year and wonder what the hell the big deal is.

They say things like…

"Hey, what the hell's the big deal? I mean eight games isn't exactly a nail-biting finish. Get over it Dad, you big crybaby!"

Well, to those of you who think us '69ers are a bunch of big crybabies who need to get over it, I say…

You weren't there, OK? You don't know what it was like. It was… it was… heartbreaking. You feel like you're driving a Lamborghini easily speeding right by everybody to the finish line, and then… cough… your engine starts sputtering… *cough*… and then you just… *cough, sputter, sputter*… run out of gas. And just then, this crappy little four-banger that has no business even being in the race speeds by you and the driver flips you off as he goes by. That's what it was like, so shut up and go to bed!

As you can see, I still harbor some anger and pain from that season that makes me lash out at people I love, but it took quite a while for me to even reach this point because, for many years, I had been living in denial. That was until my therapist, Dr. Lisa Goodbody, said that I should talk about 1969 and that I needed to let it out—all of it. The conversation went something like this:

Dr. Goodbody: *Frank, tell me all about '69.*

Me: *OK, but it'll be easier if I just show you.*

Dr. Goodbody: *No, no! The* **year** *1969.*

Me: *Oh, OK. Can I put my clothes back on first?*

While that whole incident was rather embarrassing—and nearly got me arrested—it did teach me a few very important things about myself:

1. I was so traumatized by the events of 1969 that I was indeed in denial.

2. I was using sexual innuendo as a defense mechanism.

3. Dr. Goodbody was so traumatized by my defense mechanism, she is no longer my therapist.

4. I like to number things.

But the important thing is that I am cured—I'm no longer in denial and I can face the truth of what happened that crazy summer. I've learned to accept what happened and move on with my life. Sure, I have those bad dreams—"night terrors" they call them—but I have learned to deal with those, as well. And it may be true that, in an effort to cope with accepting the past, I drink far more than I should, but the important thing is that I am no longer in denial.

So, as I continue to accept the past and move on with my life, let me share that past with you. Let me share with you the events of 1969.

Warning: What you are about to read will likely cause drug and alcohol addiction, and sexual dysfunction.

[Author's note: I just threw the sexual dysfunction thing in there for its shock value. Truthfully, reading this chapter will not cause sexual dysfunction. But the drug and alcohol addiction probably will anyway.]

1969 – Year in Review

The season started with a bang and ended with the distinct odor of poop, and in between was an emotional rollercoaster that caused me to spend years laying on couches in the fetal position, talking about my "feelings" to men with glasses, white coats, clipboards, and rectal thermometers. Yes, I may well have ended up doing that anyway, but I like to blame the Cubs for all of my mental breakdowns.

So, for those of you who get off on pain, and for those of you who just want to know why so many of us who lived through it now reside in rehab centers, here it is—a recap of the season that still has me waking up screaming obscenities in the middle of the night.

Part I - This is Way Too Easy!

April 8: It's Opening Day and Ernie Banks hits two home runs before Willie Smith belts a pinch-hit, 2-run home run in the bottom of the 11th to win the game over the Phillies 7-6. This starts the Cubs on the road to the Promised Land—assuming the Promised Land is *HELL!*

April 13: Trailing by two in the ninth, the Cubs score three to beat the Expos 7-6.

April 16-17: The Cubs win back-to-back shutouts over the Cardinals.

April 19: After knocking off the Expos in eleven innings, the Cubs' record is 10-1.

April 27: The Cubs score four in the ninth to win 8-6 and sweep a three-game series from the Mets in New York.

April Totals: 16 wins, 7 losses, two games ahead of the Pittsburgh Pirates.

May 4: After winning the first two games of the series, the Cubs get swept in a double-header against the Mets.

May 11-12: Kenny Holtzman and Ferguson Jenkins go all the way in tossing back-to-back shutouts to get the Cubs going on another roll.

May 13: The Cubs make it three straight shutouts by pounding the San Diego Padres 19-0 in one of the biggest routs in baseball history. Banks goes deep twice and drives in seven runs to lead the way.

May 16: The Cubs make it four shutouts in five games as they molest the Houston Astros 11-0 at the Astrodome. This is fun!

May 23: Dick Selma blanks the Padres giving the Cubs seven shutouts in eleven games.

May Totals: 16 wins, 9 losses.

Season record: 32 wins, 16 losses, 7 ½ games ahead of the second place Pirates.

June 6: The Cubs make it seven straight wins knocking off the Cincinnati Reds by a 14-8 score at Wrigley Field.

June 13: The Cubs rout the Reds again by a 14-8 score—this time in Cincinnati. Jimmy Qualls scores a controversial run when he leaps over Reds catcher Pat Corrales and tags home plate.

June 18: The earlier seven-game winning streak is offset by a run of five straight clunkers that culminates in a 3-2 loss at Pittsburgh. OK, what the hell is going on?

June 22: Jim Hickman's two-out, two-run homer caps a four-run ninth as the Cubs beat the Expos 7-6.

June 26: Hickman does it again, homering in the tenth to beat the Pirates 7-5.

June 29: A memorable day for all Cub fans. It is "Billy Williams Day" at Wrigley Field and the Cubs take a pair from the Cardinals. The Cubs beat old nemesis Bob Gibson 3-1 in the opener and knock the stuffings out of the dazed Redbirds 12-1 in the nightcap. Nothing better than a sweep of the Cardinals!

June 30: Banks belts one over the fence in Montreal. Everyone in the ballpark knows it except umpire Tony Venzon who says it went *under* the fence for a ground rule double. Cubs manager Leo Durocher argues and is ejected from the game. Banks loses a home run and the Cubs lose the game.

June Totals: 18 wins, 11 losses.

Season record: 50 wins, 27 losses, 7 ½ games ahead of the mildly annoying New York Mets.

July 8: In New York, the Mets come from behind to score three runs in the bottom of the ninth to beat the Cubs 4-3. In a key moment, Cubs centerfielder Don Young drops a fly ball in front of the left-centerfield wall. Following the emotional loss, Ron Santo blasts Young setting off a chorus of boos for Santo when the Cubs return to Wrigley later in the week.

July 9: There is both good news and bad news. The bad news is the Cubs lose again to the Mets making it five straight losses. The good news is that with one cut in the ninth, Qualls bangs a single to ruin crybaby Tom Seaver's attempt at a perfect game. Gee, that's a shame.

July 10: The Cubs come out on top as they beat the Mets 6-2 behind the pitching of Bill Hands. The win ends the Mets' seven-game winning streak.

July 13: A great day as the Cubs sweep a pair from the Phillies, 6-0 and 6-4.

July 14: The Cubs knock off the Mets at Wrigley Field 1-0 for their fourth straight win as Bill Hands out-duels crybaby Tom Seaver. Ron Santo clicks his heels in celebration and the crowd roars. The Mets don't like it—big babies!

July 15: It's a disappointing 5-4 loss to the Mets as slugging Mets second baseman Al Weis homers. How bad a hitter is Weis? He has just a few more career homers than my mom.

July 16: The Cubs lose again to the Mets 9-5 and again slugging Mets second baseman Al Weis smacks a home run to widen his lead over my mom. Crybaby Tom Seaver clicks his heels in celebration.

July 20: The Cubs sweep a pair in Philadelphia.

July 30: The Cubs lose, but the Mets lose a pair! I am only slightly sad.

July Totals: 15 wins, 14 losses.

Season record: 65 wins, 41 losses, 6 ½ games ahead of the still mildly annoying New York Mets.

August 6: The Cubs stretch it to seven straight wins with a 5-4 victory over the Astros in the Dome. It's getting easy again.

August 13: The Cubbies extend their lead to 8 ½ games over the Mets by knocking off the Padres 4-2. Bye-bye, Mets!

August 19: Holtzman tosses a no-hitter as he dominates the visiting Atlanta Braves in a 5-0 win. Santo pulls one onto the street with two on in the first inning to give Holtzman more runs than he needs. In the seventh inning, Billy Williams makes a memorable catch of an apparent Hank Aaron home run, and later, Holtzman gets Aaron to ground out with two outs in the ninth as Wrigley Field explodes. This is just a preview of the type of celebration the Cubs will be having in another month or so.

August 27: The Reds spank the Cubs making it seven losses in nine games since the no-hitter. WTF?

August Totals: 18 wins, 11 losses.

Season record: 83 wins, 52 losses, 4 ½ games ahead of the increasingly annoying New York Mets.

Part II - Everything Turns to Crap

Cub fans live with the understanding that, no matter how good life is right now, eventually everything turns to crap. It may sound a little pessimistic, but it comes from years of experience and it resides in the mind of even the most optimistic of Cub fans. And what occurred the last month of the 1969 season is a perfect example of the good life turning to bona fide, 100%, USDA, Grade A crap—the kind that makes your eyes bleed.

A recap of **Brown September**:

September 7: A putrid odor is already in the air, but this day begins a string of non-stop crap that will outdo all of the previous crap combined. The Cubs have already lost four in a row and have seen their lead over the Mets shrivel to 3 ½ games when they appear to be on their way to a big win over the Pirates at Wrigley Field. With a one-run lead and two outs in the ninth, Phil Regan throws a pitch that hits Willie Stargell's bat so hard that the ball eventually lands in Lake Michigan. The game is tied and, of course, the Cubs lose in extra innings.

September 8: Our heroes enter a key two-game series in New York with a slim 2 ½ game lead and the opportunity to show the Mets who is boss. The first game of the series is tied 2-2 in the sixth inning when the Mets' Tommy Agee is gunned down at the plate on a throw by Cubs' right fielder Jim Hickman. Unfortunately, plate umpire Satch Davidson, who is apparently involved in the conspiracy to change things to crap, calls Agee safe. Randy Hundley—under the mistaken impression that tagging Agee before he gets to the plate constitutes an out—jumps up and down and screams in anger. Naturally, that run is the difference in a 3-2 Cubs loss.

September 9: If, on a "sucking scale" of 1 to 10, yesterday's game is a 10, this one is about a 15. Game two of the series sucks extra bad for several reasons:

1. The Cubs are spanked 7-1.

2. Their lead in the standings is now only one-half game.

3. That goddamn black cat.

4. Man, I really *do* love to number stuff!

The thing everyone remembers about this game is that as Ron Santo stands on deck, a black cat wanders past him and walks in front of the Cubs dugout, looks directly at Leo Durocher, then walks off. The crowd cheers as the symbol for bad luck passes before the Cubs players as if to be taunting them.

September 10: The Chicago Cubs Traveling Crap Show moves on to Philadelphia where the Cubs lose to the Phillies by a 6-2 score. That, combined with a doubleheader sweep by the Mets, puts the Cubs one full game behind New York. After 155 consecutive days in first place, everything has officially turned brown.

September 11: In case anyone thinks the fall from first place is only temporary, the Cubs end any doubt as to just how bad things are on this night. The current state of affairs can be summed up in just one play from this game. With two outs in the third inning, Cubs pitcher Dick Selma has Tony Taylor picked off second base—except Selma whirls and throws the ball into left field nowhere near anyone wearing a baseball glove. Taylor scores on the play and the Cubs end up losing by a run.

September 12: Perhaps the topper of this miserable nightmare comes when the Cubs finally win, beating the Cardinals 5-1, but *still* lose ground in the standings because the Mets sweep a pair in Pittsburgh by identical 1-0 scores. And who drives in the single runs in each game? The damn Mets pitchers, that's who! The crap bus is now overflowing.

The rest of September is just more of the same, but it really doesn't matter anymore.

October 2: Good news! The Cubs beat the Mets 5-3 at Wrigley Field to move to just eight games back with zero games to go.

> *September/October Totals: 9 wins, 18 losses.*

> *Season record: 92 wins, 70 losses, 8 games back of the utterly annoying New York Mets.*

So there it is—the good, the bad, and the vomit-inducing. The Cubs made a great effort but fizzled in the end. I am told the Mets went on to beat the Atlanta Braves in the National League Championship Series and then defeated the Baltimore Orioles in the World Series. I wouldn't know. I didn't watch one lousy inning of it because it was just too nauseating.

If I seem bitter, it's only because I am. I hate the Mets! I hate black cats! And I hate 69!

Well, I hate the Mets and black cats anyway.

Chapter 14: Hey Hey Brickhead!

*F*or me and Cub fans of my generation, Jack Brickhouse is the only true voice of Chicago Cubs baseball. In fact, aside from my father, Jack spent more time in my house than any other man.

Kids in my neighborhood often referred to Brickhouse as "Brickhead"—nothing terribly mean-spirited about it, it just seemed to fit. In fact his big, bald head did look like it may have been as hard as a brick. And holy crap did we ever see a lot of that head, and not just during baseball season. At one time, in addition to being the television voice of both Cubs and White Sox baseball, Jack did Bulls basketball on WGN-TV. And in the fall, he would move to WGN radio to broadcast Bears football. Plus he often did the sports portion on WGN-TV News. The man was like herpes—you couldn't get rid of him.

I was happy to learn that the nickname "Brickhead" wasn't confined to my neighborhood. If we sat in the grandstands at Wrigley Field on the third base side, we could see members of the media walk along the catwalk as they made their way up to the press boxes. Whenever Jack appeared, fans would yell out his name and he would smile and wave down and occasionally you would hear some fans yell, "Hey Brickhead!"

In addition to feeling like a part of the family, much of Brickhouse's appeal came from the fact that he was genuine. He seemed to genuinely love the game of baseball, genuinely love the Cubs, genuinely love his job, and genuinely have fun every game—win or probably lose. And unlike today's broadcasters, when Jack was excited, he was genuinely excited—none of that made-up crap manufactured for highlight shows on ESPN.

Jack's unbridled love for the Cubs made him what some members of the media would refer to as a "homer." A homer is a guy who roots, roots, roots for the home team, and being called a homer in the sports broadcasting world is not supposed to be a compliment. Apparently broadcasting baseball games is some kind of really noble job that requires total objectivity so that we, the stupid people at home who don't know any better, are told the truth, the whole truth, and nothing but the truth. And how could a homer like Brickhouse be objective enough to point out to us stupid people at home that the Cubs really suck? Apparently last place wasn't enough evidence. But Jack didn't care about being called a "homer"—he kept on hollering "Hey Hey!" after every Cubs home run and "Oh brother!" after every Cubs misfortune. Undoubtedly, the "Oh brothers" outnumbered the "Hey Heys" most years.

Brickhouse also loved to tell us old baseball stories and anecdotes about many of the more colorful characters in baseball like Casey Stengel and Charlie Grimm—most of which we'd heard over and over and over again to the point that we would yell at the TV, "Brickhead, shut up!"

In addition to "Hey Hey!" and Oh brother!" Jack had a number of other favorite little phrases that he would use during nearly every broadcast:

Whoo, boy!

Wheeee!

Look out now.

Plenty of seats still available. So if you're in the neighborhood, it's not too late to stop by.

If we were to put this scorecard in a time capsule and dug it up years from now, nobody would be able to figure it out.

Cubs baseball brought to you in black-and-white and living color here on good old Channel 9.

Sometimes, Jack would say things that didn't even make sense—at least not to me. One of his favorites was:

There's a big difference between a batter who says 'If this pitch is a strike, I'm going to hit it,' and a batter who says 'I'm going to hit this pitch, if it's a strike.'

I never could see the difference between the two statements, other than sentence structure. Or should I say, other than sentence structure, I never could see the difference between the two statements.

For the next generation of Cub fans, Harry Caray was the voice of the Cubs. I liked Harry—he was fun to listen to and was as enthusiastic as Brickhouse. He was also responsible for bringing a lot of interest to the Cubs and a lot of fans to the ballpark. His statue outside of Wrigley Field is very cool and certainly deserved. But for thousands of Cubs fans like myself who grew up with "Brickhead" living in our houses, there is, and always will be, only one true voice of the Chicago Cubs.

Despite his annoying stories and silly phrases and unpleasant-looking head, we loved Jack in the same way you might love your uncle. He's ugly and somewhat embarrassing, but he's part of the family and you'll miss him when he's gone.

And all these years later, I miss "Brickhead."

Chapter 15: The Holy Trinity

*P*erhaps the most amazing thing about the Cubs having not appeared in a World Series since the beginning of the Big Baby Boom—or as I like to call it, the Big Mommy Bang—is the fact that for ten seasons their lineup featured three Hall of Famers batting third, fourth, and fifth every day and *still* they never got to the post-season.

Before I go on, I want you to know that I did a lot of research and math and stuff like that, which, by the way, really cut into my precious sitting around and drinking beer time, just so you could see how great this trio of hitters were during the period in which they played together. That's how much I care about you. And it's free of charge.

That trio of hitters—Ernie Banks, Billy Williams, and Ron Santo—filled the middle of the Cubs lineup from 1961 through 1970, pounding out home runs and knocking in runs like no other threesome in baseball. During that period, they combined for 799 home runs, 2,834 RBI, and a .280 batting average. That comes out to an average of 27 home runs and 94 RBI per player per year. When I think back now to Cubs teams of the 1960s, it is incredible to me that they could have three great hitters in the lineup day-in-and-day-out, year-in-and-year-out for a decade and never win a pennant of any kind. How could that be? Then I remember, hey, it's the Cubs.

Sure, other great Cubs players have come and gone. Some were probably as good if not better than any one of the three, but together Williams, Santo, and Banks made up, over an extended period of time, the greatest 3-4-5 in any batting order, of any team, in any era of Cubs baseball.

To Cub fans of my generation, they are The Holy Trinity.

Mr. Cub

"Besides Ernie Banks, who is your favorite Cubs player?" Back when I was a youngster, that was the question kids who were Cub fans would ask one another. It was understood that Ernie was everyone's favorite Cubs player. Hell, he had to be, after all, his name was "Mr. Cub."

Not only was Banks a great player, but he always looked like he was having fun. He smiled and said things like "Let's play two!" which was really something considering losing two games in one day couldn't be a hell of a lot of fun. And he did this while playing most of his career on really bad ball clubs. Through much of his career he was clearly the best player on one of baseball's worst teams, yet he never complained. There was something reassuring about Ernie to Cub fans, as if losing wasn't the worst thing in the world. It's similar to having someone on his deathbed whisper in your ear, "It's OK. Dying isn't that bad." And somehow you feel better because you think, "Well, if he can take it, so can I." So Ernie did the suffering for us and did it with a smile. For that reason we loved him.

But Banks was, first and foremost, a great hitter. Consider the six-year string he put together from 1955 through 1960, which I put into this impressive little table for you (Fig. 2, I think). I also added up the totals and calculated an average year. Once again, no charge.

Year	HR	RBI	BA
1955	44	117	.295
1956	28	85	.297
1957	43	102	.285
1958	47	129	.313
1959	45	143	.304
1960	41	117	.271
Totals	248	693	.294
Avg Yr	41	116	.294

Fig. 2, I think – Impressive Little Table

Those are some impressive little numbers in that impressive little table, don't you think? Throw in the fact that he set a National League record by belting five grand slam home runs in one season (1955), won a Gold Glove (1959), and was the first player ever named the National League's Most Valuable Player in consecutive years (1958 and 1959), and it's easy to see why Ernie was a first ballot Hall of Famer.

Many home run hitters of Banks' era were "wrist hitters" and Ernie was among the best of them. The concept was to whip the bat through the strike zone by flicking one's wrists. The stronger the hitter's wrists, the faster the bat would move and the farther the ball would travel. Power didn't come from big, muscular, juiced-up arms, like we see today, but rather from strong, supple wrists. Often it looked like the pitch was past Ernie but he would flick his wrists at the last second and the ball would jump off his bat. If he missed the ball, it looked like he had swung way late, and it wasn't pretty, but when he connected, it was a beautiful sight.

In his nineteen year career, Banks connected 512 times and if not for umpire Tony Venzon, the total would have been 513. In a 1969 game against the Montreal Expos at Jarry Park (named in honor of the late, great Jarry Park), Banks hit one that looked to everyone in the ballpark—which was roughly two-dozen Canadians with hockey sticks and missing teeth—like it cleared the right-field fence. Venzon, however, ruled the play a ground-rule double, claiming the ball went *under* the fence—quite a fete considering there were no openings under the fence. Even Expos right-fielder Rusty Staub, who had the best view of anyone, knew Venzon was full of shit. He later joked with Banks about having dug a hole. Naturally, Ernie never argued about it, he just graciously accepted the call as a double.

Many great players have come and gone wearing Cub pinstripes. Some have or will surpass Ernie's career numbers and some may even play in a World Series or two (after I'm dead, I'm sure), but there is and always will be only one "Mr. Cub."

Sweet Billy

My answer to the "Besides Ernie Banks, who is your favorite Cub player?" question was Billy Williams, the man with the sweetest swing in baseball. Even during his St. Louis broadcasting days, Harry Caray would put down his can of Budweiser long enough to tell Cardinals fans that it was worth the price of admission just to see Billy Williams swing the bat. And could he ever swing it. In his 16-year Cubs career, Williams belted 392 home runs while maintaining a .296 batting average.

Williams was the quiet Cub who let his bat do his talking for him, and when the streaky Williams was on a tear, his bat just wouldn't shut up. While Banks and Santo were hitting bombs onto Waveland Avenue, Billy, a dead pull left-handed hitter gave ball hawks a reason to scramble over to Sheffield and wait for one of his towering drives which would usually bounce high off the pavement of Sheffield and bang against the buildings across the street.

From 1962 to 1970, the steady and dependable Williams played in 1,117 consecutive games, setting what was at that time a National League record. The 1961 National League Rookie-of-the-Year played most of his early years in right field before settling in as a reliable leftfielder. Williams' steady fielding came from an intimate familiarity with the contours of Wrigley Field's outfield walls as well as an understanding of how to use the vines as a cushion while leaping against the bricks. Billy's arm, while not terribly strong, was almost always on the mark.

On a personal note, Williams had quite an influence on me. Before each at bat, Billy practiced one of baseball's most unusual rituals. As he walked to the plate from the on-deck circle, Williams would stop just before entering the batter's box and spit a wad of gum into the air. He would then take a practice cut and try to hit it. I could never really tell if Billy actually made contact with the flying gum, but I thought it was cool and tried to do it myself. Of course I wasn't very good at spitting gum in a nice high arc and it would usually end up stuck to my chin or on my shirt. On the rare occasion that I was able to let one fly, I would be so surprised that I never had a prayer of hitting it. But the good news is that I eventually got quite good at spitting out gum, so thank you Billy Williams for teaching me how to spit.

This Old Cub

Finally, more than thirty years after he first became eligible, Hall of Fame voters decided that hey, maybe that Ron Santo guy belongs in Cooperstown after all. could have told them that a long time ago when Ron was still playing and was clearly the best third baseman in the National League, but nobody asked me, so each year he didn't make it, I'd just shake my head and mutter, "What a bunch of dumbasses." It would have been nice if Ron could have actually been at his induction ceremony into the Hall of Fame, but he couldn't make it because he is DEAD!

But being overlooked was nothing new to Santo. As part of the Holy Trinity, Ron was probably the least appreciated of the three Cubs stars. While Banks was talkative, outgoing, and happy-go-lucky and Williams was quiet and dependable, Santo was emotional and outspoken, and because of that, a small contingent of Cub fans didn't like him. They recognized his talent, but to them, he was too emotional. If he was happy, Santo would jump for joy and even click his heels. If he was unhappy, he would sometimes explode, arguing with umpires and players on the other team. As team captain, he would also take it upon himself to let his own teammates have it if he thought they were dogging it. Ror Santo always left little doubt as to how he felt.

Cub fans never booed Banks and Williams—as far as the fans were concerned, those two could do no wrong. When Santo's name would be announced on the PA at Wrigley Field, there would always be a loud roar of cheers, but in the background, a soft rumble of boos could be heard. For some reason, some fans just could never warm up to him, but not so, my family. We loved Ronnie, and whenever we were at the game, we always cheered extra loud for him.

To the next generation of Cub fans, the idea of Santo ever being booed at Wrigley Field is unthinkable. That's because they have only known Ron as the loveable, befuddled Cub fan/baseball analyst who unintentionally entertained them from his perch in the radio booth for twenty-one seasons. As baseball analysts go, Santo made a great comedian. He sounded more like a drunken bleacher bum who'd just won a contest to sit in the booth for a few innings. Scorecards, players' names, and just the English language in general were all challenges for

Ron, but he always handled his struggles in the booth with a laugh. After all, this was a man who understood what *real* struggles were all about. Due to severe diabetes, he had endured numerous surgeries including amputations of both legs, quadruple heart-bypass, and removal of a tumor from his bladder. Trying to pronounce "Kosuke Fukudome" was scarcely a hardship to Santo.

It was frustrating for Cub fans who loved Santo, who remembered him as a great player, who laughed at the crazy things he said in the radio booth, who suffered along with him through each surgery and procedure, to see how the Hall of Fame veterans committee would turn him away year after year. We all knew how badly he wanted it and it hurt to realize that this man who had already lived decades beyond his life expectancy wasn't going to be around forever. With each year, the likelihood that Ron would live to see the day that he was finally accepted into the Hall of Fame diminished. And, of course he never did live to see it.

But now, at last, Santo has joined his old teammates Banks and Williams in baseball's hallowed Hall of Fame. The Holy Trinity is once again whole.

Part Three: Rounding Third

Trivia and Other Crap

*Q*uick! What was the greatest game the Cubs have ever played? How about the worst? Which manager was fired during spring training? Who shot Eddie Waitkus? Which Cubs teams sucked the worst? Who are my fifty favorite Cub players since 1960? And who is number one on my enemies list? You will find the answers to these and many other burning questions right here.

Chapter 16: A Dozen Reasons Wrigley Rules

Sure it's kind of falling apart and the bathrooms are pretty disgusting and there's no parking, but it's the ultimate place to watch a baseball game.

Built in 1914 for the Chicago Whales, the ballpark located at Clark and Addison streets became the home of the Cubs two years later when the Federal League folded. Now, nearly a century later, Wrigley Field is a baseball shrine visited by more than three million fans each year.

Here are a dozen reasons Wrigley Field is a place every baseball fan should visit at least once before passing on to that big ballpark in the sky.

#1: The Name

A majority of the ballparks built over the past twenty years have been named after big corporations—some infamous (does Enron Field ring a bell?)—more than willing to pay lots of bucks so they can have their names attached to sports stadiums. And in an economy where fans are desperately trying to scrape enough dough together to take their kids to the ballgame, a large number of stadiums are named after banks. The Cubs could no doubt co the same and receive an enormous check in return, but more than thirty years after the Wrigley family sold the Cubs, the name lives on.

#2: The Scoreboard

Forget the Green Monster at Fenway Park—Wrigley has a green monster of its own.

The massive, manually operated scoreboard sits high above the centerfield bleachers and provides everything you need, including inning-by-inning scores of the out-of-town games. The flags of each of the National League teams sit atop the scoreboard giving everyone a clear idea of the strength and direction of the all-important wind (see #4 below). And after each game a flag is flown indicating to passersby how the Cubs fared that day. If the Cubs win, a white flag with a blue W flies proudly. Following a loss, it's a blue flag with a white L.

The blue flag sucks.

#3: The Ivy

The ivy is what makes Wrigley Field the most recognizable ballpark in the National League, and the fact that Bill Veeck is the one who planted it way back in 1937 means it should be regarded as hallowed vegetation. In the spring, the ivy looks brown and dead; in the summer, it looks green and healthy; and in the fall (a time Cub fans rarely get a glimpse), it looks beautifully colorful. But does the ivy look good enough to eat?

Back in the '70s, WGN cameras caught Cubs outfielder Jose Cardenal eating the ivy while his team changed pitchers. Actually, no one was really surprised by Jose's strange behavior. Fans who remember Cardenal may recall that he once missed a game because he claimed his eyelid was stuck shut.

#4: The Wind

Wind is a factor in every game at Wrigley Field. If the wind is blowing out, you'll probably see a slugfest and if it's blowing in, expect a pitcher's duel. A swirling wind could mean players colliding as they chase pop-ups. And if the wind isn't blowing at all, check your surroundings because you're probably sitting in the wrong ballpark.

#5: The Rooftops

The rooftops along Waveland and Sheffield truly have become a part of the ballpark and it almost doesn't look like there are streets that run between the buildings and the bleachers. Most days, the rooftops are more heavily populated (Fig. 3) than US Comiskey Cellular Park Field II is whenever the White Sox are in town.

Fig. 3 - There are actually more fans in this picture than at your average White Sox game

#6: The Bullpens

At Wrigley Field, the bullpens are located out beyond the dugouts between the foul lines and the stands, which allows fans to easily see who is warming up—and steal souvenirs.

In a May, 2000 game against L.A., a fan reached over the wall and snatched the hat off Dodgers catcher Chad Kreuter's fat head as Kreuter sat on the bullpen bench. The fan took off running and Kreuter—apparently feeling an unusually strong affection for his hat—climbed into the stands to try to retrieve it. A fight ensued with several fans eventually getting tossed from the ballpark.

You're just not gonna get to see that kind of fun anywhere but at Wrigley.

#7: The Marquee

The red marquee at the front entrance of the ballpark proudly welcomes visitors and also keeps them up-to-date on the latest Cubs news. Or, if you give them a few bucks, they'll even make up shit for you (Fig. 4).

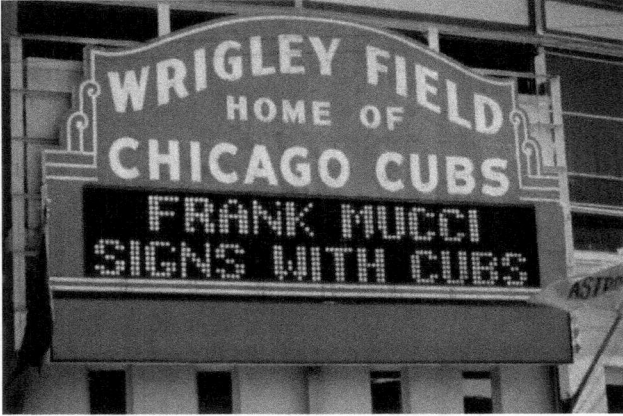

Fig. 4 - Some shit they made up for me

#8: Kenmore Ave.

The two streets that run along the left and right field walls are Waveland and Sheffield and both have seen plenty of home runs over the years. The final resting place of two of the longest home runs ever hit at Wrigley, however, was on Kenmore which runs perpendicular off of Waveland.

In 1976, Cubs slugger Dave Kingman hit one that rolled down Kenmore and traveled an estimated 530 feet. In 2003, Sammy Sosa nearly matched Kingman's fete with a 520 foot Kenmore blast.

#9: The Bleachers

Still the best seats in the house, the bleachers at Wrigley Field are where it's at if you want to catch home run balls, sun bathe, check out girls, or yell obscenities and hurl things at the other team.

Back in the late '60s and early '70s, the left-field bleachers were home to the Bleacher Bums—a collection of mainly college kids who attended every home game, wore helmets, did cheers, and basically terrorized opposing outfielders. It was the Bums' rowdy behavior that led to the installation of...

#10: The Baskets

The baskets just above the ivy at the tops of the outfield walls were first installed during the 1970 season after a particularly rowdy series of games. The wire baskets were erected in an effort to keep bleacherites from jumping down onto the field and throwing trash at the opposition.

The baskets not only help discourage rowdiness, but increase the number of home runs hit at Wrigley—good for hitters but bad news for pitchers like Ferguson Jenkins who used to refer to the baskets as "homer catchers."

#11: The Posts

Back when Wrigley Field was built, ballpark engineers believed that the best way to keep the upper deck from crashing down and killing people was to hold it up with posts, which proved to be a pretty good idea. Apparently today's engineers are a whole lot smarter than those guys, because they've figured out a way to build upper tiers without using posts thus giving fans an unobstructed view of the field.

That's nice, but I think the posts provide a look from the past that the new ballparks are sorely missing. Plus I like the idea that people actually buy those "obstructed view" seats and are willing to sit behind a post and peek around either side of it to see what's going on. Kind of adds to the charm, don't you think?

#12: The 'Hood

Cub fans like to drink—a century of losing will do that to you. Luckily we don't have to go far to find a place to help us forget about that ninth inning two-base throwing error and salvage some fun out of the day. Before, during, and after games, the drinking and eating establishments throughout Wrigleyville are overflowing with fans drunk enough to believe the Cubs will climb out of the cellar and win the pennant.

That requires some big time drinking, folks!

And Half-a-Dozen Things I Miss...

Whoop Boom!

Until the '80s, Wrigley Field had a screen behind home plate that angled upward to the upper deck. When foul balls hit behind the plate came down, they would land on the screen and roll downward before dropping onto the field where the batboy would retrieve them. As the ball rolled down the screen, fans would simultaneously let out a long "Whooooop!" which would continue until the ball reached the end of the screen. Then when it fell to the ground, everyone would respond with a loud "Boom!"

Sadly, the screen was replaced with one that stands straight up and so now we have an entire generation of Cub fans who have never experienced the joy of whoop-booming.

Paper Cups

Concession drinks at Wrigley Field used to be served in paper cups, which have since been replaced by plastic ones. The sad thing about that is fans no longer get to hear the sound of paper cups popping. Following every game at Wrigley, kids would collect the empty paper cups lying around the seats, turn them over, and stomp on them. During The Tenth Inning show on WGN, Jack Brickhouse would be up in the booth interviewing one of the ballplayers and in the background you could hear the popping sounds of smashed paper cups.

It's the closest we Cub fans have ever come to hearing the sound of popping champagne corks in a World Series-winning clubhouse.

The Catwalks

Running from the grandstands to the bleachers in both left and right field were catwalks that allowed vendors and ushers to easily gain entry to and from the bleachers. Many a home run ball would hit those concrete catwalks and bounce high off the screened fences behind them before bounding back out onto the field.

Those catwalks have since been replaced by seats and the right field section is now a Budweiser party patio. So now most of the cats you see walking out there are drunk.

Have Your Pencils and Scorecards Ready...

For nearly a thousand years, the Cubs' public address announcer was an old fellow named Pat Peiper. Prior to each game, he would tell fans in a raspy, monotone voice to "Have your pencils and scorecards ready and I will give you the correct lineups for today's ballgame." Each name would be announced without any emotion or embellishment. Just the facts—all he gave us were the facts.

The starting lineups are still given before each game, but it's done with that typical cheerful, fake, annoying voice PA announcers use now that makes you want to throw up your hotdog and Frosty Malt.

I miss the grouchy old man approach to public address announcing.

Sunshine

One of the things that made Wrigley Field special was that a half century after night baseball was introduced to the major leagues, it was the only ballpark without lights. The Cubs still schedule more day games than any other team, but that number is slowly dwindling and will likely grow smaller and smaller until the Cubs are playing as many night games as everyone else.

Sure, the toll of playing all those games in the hot sun probably contributed to the Cubs' late-season collapse in 1969, but at least the players—and the fans—had nice, healthy-looking tans.

Cigars

I'm not a big fan of the smell of cigars, but whenever I get a whiff of one it brings back memories of being a kid at Wrigley Field. That's because back before smoking in public became a major crime, there were always old men at the ballpark chomping on cigars, reading the sports section from the morning paper, and bitching at the Cubs.

Old men still bitch at the Cubs, but now they'll live to be even older because their lungs are smoke-free.

Chapter 17: Who's In Charge Here?

*T*he Cubs have had roughly one million managers since they last appeared in a World Series. That's just an estimate, but being the kind of guy who likes to have all his facts straight, I'm gonna grab a beer or two, go online, and find out exactly how many managers the Cubs have had since 1945. Be right back…

Sorry that took so long but I got a little distracted. That's what happens if you accidentally Google search "Kate Upton cat daddy video" when you mean to enter "Chicago Cubs managers" and then you accidentally play the video in a loop for a couple hours. Common error.

Anyway, between the years 1945 (the last year the Cubs appeared in a World Series, in case you're stupid) and 2012, the Cubs have had exactly 37 managers. That's not a million, but it's still a lot. My amazing math skills tell me that comes out to an average tenure of about 1.8 years per manager. Pretty tough gig, I'd say.

So I decided to go through and take a look at each of these fine men and see what kinds of geniuses we Cub fans have been blessed with over the years. I don't remember anything about the Cubs prior to the 1960s, so I've had to rely on my favorite g-rated website, BaseballReference.com, to help me out.

You go ahead and read. I'm gonna go accidentally check out Kate's video again.

Manager (1945-1960)

Charlie Grimm (1945-1949, 1960)

The last manager to take the Cubs to the World Series, it would be wonderful to ask "Jolly Cholly" all about what it's like to lead a team into the Fall Classic, but we can't because he's been dead for more than a quarter-of-a-century. With 900-plus wins as a manager and pennants in '32, '35, and '45, this man was way too successful to be on this list of losers.

Frankie Frisch (1949-1951)

Frisch was a Hall of Fame ballplayer who also had some success as a manager—unfortunately that success was not with the Cubs. In twelve-plus seasons as manager of the Cardinals and Pirates, Frisch's winning percentage was an excellent .530. His two-and-a-half years with the Cubs, however, produced a putrid .418 winning percentage.

Phil Cavarretta (1951-1953)

One of the greatest Cub players of all time, Cavarretta's managerial career came to an abrupt end a few days before the '54 season was to start. Cubs' owner Phil Wrigley was not happy with Cavarretta's comments to a reporter about his team being little more than a big pile of crap and fired him. Cavarretta was so upset over his firing he completely lost his head and signed with the White Sox. Phil, there are better ways to deal with life's setbacks—excessive drinking is one that comes to mind.

Stan Hack (1954-1956)

Hack, another excellent Cub player, replaced Cavarretta and quickly learned that Phil may have underestimated the crap level of his team. They finished in seventh place with a 64-90 record, and two years later, Hack would lead the Cubs to an even worse 60-94 season.

Bob Scheffing (1957-1959)

Like Frisch, Scheffing found out that the Cubs and success just aren't a good fit. His winning percentage in three years as Cubs manager: .450; his winning percentage in three years with the Detroit Tigers: .548.

Lou Boudreau (1960)

Poor Lou—a World Series winning manager with Cleveland and a future Hall of Famer—was retired and enjoying life up in the Cubs radio booth. Barely a month into the '60 season, he was asked to trade places with then-manager Charlie Grimm—the first ever broadcaster-for-manager swap in baseball history. How bad was it? After the season Boudreau was fired and replaced by the ill-conceived... wait for it...

College of Coaches (1961-1965)

Vedie Himsl (1961)

The first head coach in baseball history, after all these years, Himsl's career 10-21 record st ll puts him at the top of the list of greatest managers of all time named Vedie.

Harry Craft (1961)

Craft wasn't around long enough to really screw things up. Sure, his 7-9 record was a very Cub-like sub-.500, but at that time 7-9 was pretty damn good. It wasn't until later that he proved he was Cub material leading Houston to a .409 winning percentage in three seasons.

El Tappe (1961-1962)

His name sounds like it might be Spanish for "the rug," but actually El Tappe is English for "Another Cubs manager with a losing record." Want proof? How about 46-70, .397?

Lou Klein (1961-1962, 1965)

Klein, after earlier stints as head coach, took over at mid-season of '65 for Bob Kennedy and has the distinction of being the last-ever head coach in Major League history. That is unless some other owner suffers major brain damage and the "College of Coaches" idea is ever reinstated.

Charlie Metro (1962)

I don't remember Charlie Metro and my research shows why. Under his watch, the Cubs won 43 and lost 69. Thankfully, his watch ended when the season ended.

Bob Kennedy (1963-1965)

The only full-time head coach, Kennedy gave the Cubs their lone winning season during the "college" era with an 82-80 record in '63. That should be enough to put him in the Cubs Hall of Fame.

Back to the Manager Thing (1966-present)

Leo Durocher (1966-1972)

After five years without a manager, Wrigley hired the man who would go on to win the most games (535) of any Cubs manager of the post-World War II era. Under Durocher, the Cubs became a contender unfortunately best known for one of baseball's biggest collapses in 1969.

Whitey Lockman (1972-1974)

The more he stuck around, the worse he got. Lockman took over for Durocher after Leo was fired in mid-'72. The team responded by going 39-26—a sparkling .600 winning percentage—and finished in second place. In '73, the Cubs dropped to 77-84 and fifth place, and the following year, they were in last place when Lockman was booted out the door.

Jim Marshall (1974-1976)

When you think about Jim Marshall, think "consistency." After finishing up for Lockman in '74, Marshall posted back-to-back 75-87 records. Apparently, Cub management wasn't looking for that kind of consistency and sent him packing.

Herman Franks (1977-1979)

Franks holds the distinction of leading the San Francisco Giants to four straight second place finishes back when there were no divisions and the league was a ten-team race (1965-1968). As manager of the Cubs, Franks could only *dream* of second place.

Joe Amalfitano (1979, 1980-1981)

After many years of coaching and quietly waiting his turn, Joe was rewarded with the thankless task of managing one of the worst collections of Cub players ever assembled, which is saying a lot. His record: 66 wins, 116 losses.

Preston Gomez (1980)

I had completely forgotten that Gomez had ever been a Cubs manager. Then I looked at the numbers (38-52) and realized why.

Lee Elia (1982-1983)

What the fuck can you say about Lee Elia that hasn't already been fuckin' said?

Charlie Fox (1983)

As interim manager, Fox was given the job of trying to clean up the mess Elia started. He made it messier with a 17-22 record.

Jim Frey (1984–1986)

He led the Cubs to a first place finish in '84, ending a 39-year drought, and brought the Cubs to within a whisker of the World Series. JUST ONE STINKING WIN AWAY!!!

John Vukovich (1986)

He managed just two games as interim manager, winning one and losing one. You would think a .500 record would have earned Vukovich a long-term contract.

Gene Michael (1986-1987)

Michael managed like he hit. Career Batting Average: .229. Any questions?

Frank Lucchesi (1987)

Lucchesi was named interim manager for the final twenty-five games of '87. His 8-17 record suggests "interim" was a good decision.

Don Zimmer (1988-1991)

"Popeye" represented the embodiment of a baseball lifer—a guy who eats, sleeps, and drinks baseball. And what an embodiment he had in those stretchy double-knit uniforms the Cubbies had back then. The unexpected first-place finish in '89 still goes down as one of the great managing jobs ever in Cubs history.

Joe Altobelli (1991)

Altobelli (Italian for "high stomach"?) served as the Cubs' interim manager for just one game (0-1). You would think the guy who had won a World Series as manager of the Baltimore Orioles in 1983 would have gotten more of a chance than that. I mean Jim Essian for crying out loud?!

Jim Essian (1991)

The former White Sox catcher took over for Zimmer and by the end of the year Cub management couldn't wait to tell him, "Nah, nah, hey, hey, goodbye."

Jim LeFebvre (1992-1993)

His big mistake was leading the Cubs to a winning record of 84-78 in 1993. Unfamiliar with even moderate success, Cub management let LeFebvre go and replaced him with the far more comfortable Tom Trebelhorn.

Tom Trebelhorn (1994)

The Cubs broke a long-standing rule of never hiring a guy named after a musical instrument. Trebelhorn's one year as manager—cut short by a player strike—produced a record of 49-64, reminding everyone why that musical instrument rule was instituted in the first place.

Jim Riggleman (1995-1999)

"Riggs" was the anti-Zimmer. Lean and muscular, he looked so good in his perfectly-tailored uniform, Cub management kept him around longer than any manager since Durocher. Riggleman's last three years were like a roller-coaster: 58-94, 90-73, 67-95. After that last showing, management decided looks aren't everything.

Don Baylor (2000-2002)

Baylor never smiled. He was one Cubs manager who seemed to take this losing stuff really hard.

Rene Lachemann (2002)

After managing only one game (a loss) in an interim role, Lachemann was replaced by Bruce Kimm.

Bruce Kimm (2002)

Despite the whole Jim Essian experience, the Cubs decided to give the former White Sox catcher idea another shot. Again, it didn't work. I think it's time to get a rule in the books about never, ever hiring an ex-White Sox catcher before they do it again.

Dusty Baker (2003-2006)

Baker made an immediate impact by taking a team that had lost 95 games the previous year and bringing them to within a whisker of the World Series. JUST FIVE STINKING OUTS!!! Then everything turned to crap and it wasn't long before Cub fans were booing and management was saying "Adios dude!"

Lou Piniella (2007-2010)

When he was awake, Lou was a pretty good manager. His first two years brought back-to-back divisional titles. His last two years brought plenty of time for long naps.

Mike Quade (2010-2011)

If he could manage as well as he could come up with nicknames for his players, he'd be in the Hall of Fame. Unfortunately, "Cassy," "Sori,"

"Wellsey," "Rammy," and the gang couldn't catchy, throwy, hitty, or winny and Quade was left looking for a jobby.

Dale Sveum (2012-present)

The first manager of the Theo Epstein era, Sveum hopes to still be around once the rebuilding is complete and the Cubs have players who can catch, throw, hit, and win. Stay tuned...

Chapter 18: Useless Crap

*F*or nearly fifty years, my alcohol-impaired brain has accumulated a large amount of useless crap from Cubs history and it wants out! So here now, for your pleasure, is a list of all kinds of Cubbie information that is sure to wow your friends at parties—assuming you go to parties at which drugs and alcohol are consumed in enormous quantities.

What's in a Name?

This may be hard to believe, but way back in the 1800s, the Cubs were originally called the White Stockings. After the turn of the century, they came to their senses and changed to the Cubs leaving the lame notion of naming your team after foot apparel to the south side.

Sure He Was a Prick, But He Was a Successful Prick

Word is that Cap Anson was a racist who played a key role in making sure the game stayed white long before Jackie Robinson came along. He was, however, the first great player in Cubs history and managed the Cubs to several championships back in the late 1800s. Did you hear that? *SEVERAL* championships! The Cubs! Several championships!

If Only His Name Had Been Saturday Night

From 1883 to 1887, the Cubs had a young outfielder who would eventually gain fame, not for his ability to hit a baseball, but rather for his "fire-and-brimstone" sermons. By 1903, Billy Sunday had given up baseball to become a pain-in-the-ass evangelist who ranted and raved about the evils of booze, thus playing a major role in America's adoption of Prohibition in 1919.

Thankfully, the Eighteenth Amendment was repealed in 1933 and we Americans were allowed to once again drink ourselves silly and go on with our lives.

West Side Groundsville

The Cubs haven't always been located on the north side of Chicago. After playing in a number of different parks throughout the city (including one called South Side Park!), the Cubs settled in at what was known as West Side Grounds—which was located at Polk and Lincoln streets—way back in 1893. West Side Grounds was home during the glory years of the early 1900s and it wasn't until 1916 that the Cubs became permanent residents of Wrigleyville.

He Hate me!

The Cubs' legendary double-play combination of the early part of the twentieth century was made up of shortstop Joe Tinker, second baseman Johnny Evers, and first baseman Frank Chance. Despite playing side-by-side for years, Tinker and Evers despised each other and for several seasons never said a word to one another.

Seeing as how the Cubs won four pennants in five years during that period, it looks like we can officially say that all this "team chemistry" crap we always hear about is just a flaming pile of poop.

Don't Give Him the Finger

Mordecai Three Finger Brown is proof that having a digit amputated by farming equipment isn't necessarily a bad thing. It seems missing a finger allowed Brown to put an unusual spin on the ball which helped make him one of the greatest pitchers of all time.

Conversely, former Cub pitcher Antonio Alfonseca is proof that having an *extra* finger isn't necessarily a *good* thing.

No runs, No hits, No win

On May 2, 1917, Cubs left-hander Jim "Hippo" Vaughn and Reds hurler Fred "Apparently Not a Hippo" Toney combined to produce the only double no-hitter (both teams hitless through nine innings) in baseball history. The Reds finally recorded a hit and scored a run in the tenth inning and—this will shock you!—the Cubs lost.

Throw the Ball to Charlie!

The Cubs' 1919 ball club had an infield that included Charlie Pick at second base, Charlie Hollocher at shortstop, and Charlie Deal at third base. It must have been confusing at times.

With Gilligan, the Skipper Too... ♫

Beginning in 1922, the Cubs' spring training home for most of the next thirty years was an island located twenty miles off the coast of southern California. William Wrigley, part-owner of Catalina Island (When do you know you have lots of money? When you own an island!), decided to build a ballpark on it. Each spring, Cubs players would ferry over to the island for a couple of months of sun and fun before embarking on the disappointment of another miserable baseball season.

Yeah, But Does This Wrigley Field Have Parking?

In 1925, William Wrigley built a ballpark in Los Angeles to house the minor league team he had purchased just a few years earlier. Named Wrigley Field, the ballpark was home to the Pacific Coast League's Los Angeles Angels (literal translation: The Angels Angels) for many years. When L.A. was awarded an American League franchise in 1961, the new team—also called The Angels Angels—occupied Wrigley Field for its first season.

The ballpark, designed to look like Chicago's Wrigley Field, was also used as the backdrop for many old movies and was home of the popular Home Run Derby TV show back in 1959 and 1960.

Going, Going, Drunk!

Hack Wilson was short and stocky and loved to get drunk. I'm short and stocky and love to get drunk too, but I could never hit a baseball like he could. For 68 years, Wilson held the National League record for home runs with 56 until the use of performance-enhancing pharmaceuticals became the norm in 1998.

Wilson, however, still holds the major league mark for RBI in a single season with 191, and for shots of whiskey in a single night with 46.

The Homer in the What?

Hall of Fame catcher Gabby Hartnett hit the most famous home run in Cubs history. In the ninth inning of a game against the Pirates during the 1938 pennant race, it was getting kind of dark outside when Hartnett belted what will forever be known as "The Homer in the Gloamin'." The home run won the crucial game for the Cubs and ultimately the pennant.

In case you were wondering, "gloamin'" is actually a lazy version of the word "gloaming," which means "kind of dark." But I guess "The Homer in the Kind of Dark" would sound pretty stupid.

Let There Be Dark

Speaking of playing baseball in the "kind of dark," in 1941, Phil Wrigley was planning to have lights installed at his ballpark. Then, the Japanese bombed Pearl Harbor and Wrigley donated the materials to the war effort because apparently the military had a greater need for night baseball than did the Cubs.

Near-Fatal Attractions

What is it with Cubs players and crazy-assed women with guns?

During the 1932 season, Billy Jurges was shot twice in his hotel room by Violet Valli. The woman said that she had done it for love, which makes you wonder what she might have done for hate.

Seventeen years later, Phillies first baseman and ex-Cub, Eddie Waitkus, was shot in the chest by crazy 19-year-old Ruth Steinhagen in a Chicago hotel room. The young lady, who for years had been obsessed with the ballplayer, was so upset Waitkus had been traded away from the Cubs, she decided if she couldn't have Eddie, nobody would. Yes, she had done it for love too. Like Jurges, Waitkus recovered from his injuries.

Throw the Damn Ball!

In the ninth inning of a 1949 game between the Cubs and Cardinals, Chicago centerfielder Andy Pafko made a shoe-top grab of a sinking liner by Rocky Nelson with two outs, one runner on base, and the Cubs leading 3-2. Umpire Al Barlick ruled that the ball hit the ground. As Pafko raced in to argue the call with the ball securely in his possession, the base runners, including Nelson, circled the bases for the winning runs.

Right there, encapsulated in one play, is pretty much what it's like to be a Cub fan. I mean does this crap happen to other teams?

"Smelly" Smalley

For most of his career at Wrigley Field (1948-1953), shortstop Roy Smalley heard lots of boos from Cub fans. Part of the reason was no doubt due to the fact that he was a .227 lifetime hitter. The rest of the reason was that he couldn't field worth a crap either. In 1950, Smalley committed a mind-boggling 51 errors! There's no information as to whether or not Smalley actually used a glove.

A Sound Hitting Approach

Most pitchers are lousy hitters, but back in the '60s Cubs hurler Bob Buhl was so bad he decided to take up switch-hitting. But Buhl's decision to switch-hit had nothing to do with making him a better hitter. He simply chose to bat from whichever side of the plate was closest to the Cubs' dugout so he'd have a shorter walk back to the bench after striking out.

If Only He Could Have Hypnotized the Batters

Bill Faul pitched for the Cubs in the mid-'60s and, for a while, looked like a star in the making. During the '65 season, Faul, equipped with a blazing fastball, recorded three shutouts in just sixteen starts. Faul credited his success that year to self-hypnosis—before each start, he would put himself into a trance. The following year, Faul won just one game and his career was pretty much over. Apparently, the opposing hitters weren't buying all that hypnosis crap.

Mrs. Meyers, Can Lee Come Out and Play?

In 1966, 19-year-old Cubs minor league pitcher, Lee Meyers, married 35-year-old Hollywood bombshell, Mamie Van Doren. The marriage ended in '67 when Van Doren grew tired of having to drive Meyers to all of his games.

Yeah, I made that part up. I don't know why they divorced, but I bet it would make a great *E! True Hollywood Story*.

Pass the Salt

Following the 1975 season, Phil Wrigley made another one of his "what the fuck is he doing?" decisions and promoted E. R. "Salty" Saltwell to the position of Cubs general manager. Saltwell had, of course, earned this lofty spot after years of being manager of park operations, which I guess means he made sure the ballpark was operating well. General Manager, however, is a whole different thing. Since the G.M. is in charge of making sure the team is operating well, he has to know baseball talent when he sees it. After just one season, Saltwell was back in charge of ordering peanuts and Frosty Malts.

He's Heavy and He's My Brother

On August 21, 1975, Rick and Paul Reuschel teamed up to blank the Los Angeles Dodgers by a 7-0 score. This marked the first time in major league history brothers had combined for a shutout.

At about 250 pounds apiece, the two also set the record for the most combined weight by brothers in one game, breaking the old record held by Felipe, Matty, and Jesus Alou.

A Hill of a Blast!

Until May 11, 2000, no one had ever expected to catch a home run ball on any of the rooftops beyond the bleachers. That's the night Glenallen Hill hit a majestic home run that came down on the roof of a three-story building on Waveland Ave. The blast was credited as having traveled just 490 feet, which prompted Cubs first-baseman Mark Grace to declare, "Four-ninety? That was 790!"

Seventh Inning STENCH!

Ever since Harry Caray checked into that great broadcast booth in the sky, the Cubs have had guest singers lead the crowd in *Take Me Out To The Ballgame* during the seventh inning stretch. Many famous to semi-famous celebrities have had the opportunity to show the world that singing should be restricted to humans. The worst of all time, however, was a man who makes a living at singing.

During the 2003 season, Ozzy Osbourne and his wife Sharon graced the broadcast booth with their presence and proceeded to butcher one of the most famous songs in American history. Ozzy, barely running on his three remaining drug-and-alcohol-free brain cells, had no idea what the words were, or what the tune was for that matter. Sharon did her best to hold things together (and Ozzy up), but the damage had already been done.

It was, however, very entertaining in a train wreck kind of way.

You Take Him, No You Take Him

On September 22, 1987, the Cubs traded pitcher Dickie Noles to the Detroit Tigers for a player to be named later. A month later, Noles was returned to the Cubs as the player to be named later.

As usual, the Cubs got screwed.

Chapter 19: The Worst of the Worst

*W*e Cub fans are a resilient bunch. No other team has fans that bounce back from disastrous seasons year-after-year like we do. The Cubs have had more than their share of miserable seasons in the past half century, but listed below, in chronological order, are ten seasons that really tested the loyalty of even the die-hardiest Cub fans. Some were horrible years that made you want to puke and others were just gut-wrenchingly disappointing and led to binge-drinking. I have to admit that there were a ton of crappy years from which to choose and, after a lot of consideration, some—aw hell, who am I kidding?—*many* worthy contenders had to be eliminated from the list.

Warning: What you are about to read may make you sick.

1960

This year was so bad that two all-time great managers, Charlie Grimm and Lou Boudreau, couldn't fix it. In fact, it was so absolutely terrible that neither Grimm nor Boudreau ever managed again—they'd had enough. How bad was it? It inspired the ill-advised "College of Coaches" idea. As a matter of fact, it was so incredibly awful Congress considered passing legislation barring children from attending Cubs games. Or at least they should have.

There was this one highlight however: On May 15 in his first appearance as a Cub, newly acquired pitcher Don Cardwell tossed a no-hitter against the Cardinals at Wrigley Field. Eventually, Cardwell settled down and started pitching the way a Cubs pitcher is supposed to pitch, going 7-14 with a 4.37 ERA the remainder of the season.

1962

The first ever 100-loss season (59-103) for the Cubs, this was year two of the doomed "College of Coaches" experiment. Everyone should have had a pretty good idea of how the season would go after the Cubs lost in Houston on opening day to the expansion Colt .45s—the first team ever named after a malt liquor—by a score of 11-2. The Cubbies were swept by the newcomers and went on to lose nine of their first ten games. The fabulous trio of El Tappe, Lou Klein, and Charlie Metro did their head-coachingest best, but our heroes just couldn't get things together.

1966

The initial season of the Leo Durocher era, the Cubs responded to their new manager with yet another 103 loss season. Despite the terrible record, Durocher was in the process of building a team that would contend for a couple of pennants over the next several years including the '69 ball club that would crash and burn and break our hearts. Never-the-less, the '66 season was a disaster even by Cubs standards.

Not that there weren't highlights that year. On July 20, Cubs outfielder Byron Browne struck out three times giving him a National League record eight strikeouts in two games. Browne, showing his two-game total was no fluke, went on to fan 143 times that year.

1974

Following a disappointing 77-84 finish in '73, it became apparent that many of the stars who had made up the Cubs roster for the last decade, were now well past their prime. So the Cubs cleaned house by trading away Ron Santo, Glenn Beckert, Randy Hundley, Jim Hickman, and Ferguson Jenkins. Unfortunately, the house got even dirtier after guys like George Mitterwald, Vic Harris, Bill Bonham and the aptly named Steve Swisher moved in. The final record was a very messy 66 wins, 96 losses and it was time to clean house again.

1980

The first of two consecutive "Holy crap do we suck!" years, this team featured such stars as Mike Tyson (not the boxer), Jesus Figueroa (not the savior), and Barry Foote (not good). The highlight of the season came on July 25 when cranky, old manager Preston Gomez was fired and replaced by fan-favorite Joe Amalfitano. Unfortunately for Joe, the players stayed.

1981

The good news was the strike! Thanks to a mid-season player strike, 59 games were erased from the Cubs' schedule. Had they played those games at the same pace as the 103 games they did play (38-65), the Cubbies would have had a sparkling record of 60 wins, 102 losses.

The Cubs started the season a tad sluggishly losing thirteen of their first fourteen games. Then they went on a tear winning nine of their next thirty-two to improve their record to 10-36. When the strike began, the Cubs' record was a dismal 15-37. There was no hope.

But wait! The owners decided after the strike was over to have a second season using the remainder of the schedule. Every team would start fresh with 0-0 records. The teams in first place when the strike began would be first-half champions. The first place winners from the second half would then play them for the divisional championship. So the Cubbies were able to wipe the slate clean and start over. They were much improved during the second season, going 23-28, but that just wasn't enough to win the division.

Perhaps a second strike and a third mini-season would have done the trick, but we'll never know.

1985

The Cubs have had worse records than the 77-84 they posted in '85, but few as disappointing. Coming off the Eastern Division title of '84, big things were expected, and it looked like big things were coming. On June 11, the Cubs were securely in first place with a record of 35-19. Then the injuries started piling up—every starting pitcher made at least one trip to the disabled list—and thirteen straight losses later, the Cubs were in fourth place and pretty much out of it. What had been the best team in the National League for the past 215 games (131-84) was suddenly a mess and would never recover.

When people ask why Cub fans savor each victory, this is the reason: Cubs dominance is ever so fleeting.

1994

Thankfully, this was another strike-shortened season and it saved the Cubs from yet another 90-loss campaign (49-64). What kind of year was it? Cubs centerfielder Karl "Tuffy" Rhodes whacked three home runs off Dwight Gooden on opening day and the Cubs *still* lost, 12-8. Then Rhodes, in true Cub-like fashion, went on to belt just five more homers the rest of the year.

1997

It's hard to imagine that there could be any good news in a season that starts with thirteen straight losses, but there is if you really look for it. And I found it! In spite of the terrible start, the Cubs managed to somehow avoid 100 losses. In fact, their record was an almost respectable (if you think thirteen games under .500 is almost respectable) 68-81 the remainder of the season.

Chapter 20: The Worst Game Ever Played

*T*uesday, September 16, 1975: A date that shall live in infamy.

That morning, 4,932 innocent people woke up completely unaware that later that day they would together bear witness to the worst game ever played in the history of the Chicago Cubs.

To fully appreciate the enormity of that statement, you must realize that in 1975, the Chicago National League franchise was celebrating its 100th year of playing baseball. And you can be sure that in a century of ballgames, the Cubs had played their fair share of crappy ones by the time those fans—oblivious to what they would soon see—headed to Wrigley Field. Hell, just the previous day, the Cubs had lost 9-1—that couldn't have been too pretty!—but a pounding like that would have felt like a World Series win compared to what would happen that afternoon.

As they prepared to make the trek to Wrigley Field that day, some of the fans were no doubt looking forward to enjoying a relaxing afternoon of sun and fun at the ballpark. Among them were probably kids too excited to sleep the night before as they anticipated going to their first baseball game—their sweet innocence soon to be defiled and destroyed by men they had misguidedly decided to idolize.

As excited as these Cub fans may have been, it's fair to say most of them probably weren't expecting a victory—the first place Pittsburgh Pirates were in town and this 1975 version of the Cubs wasn't any damn good—but no one could have expected the carnage that was about to take place. After all, the Cubs had their best pitcher, Rick Reuschel, on the mound. How bad could it be?

Then the game started and everyone found out it could be really, really awful.

Some of the more astute fans probably recognized early on that Reuschel didn't quite have his best stuff when the first nine Pirate batters in succession: doubled, singled, walked, singled, hit a sacrifice fly, singled, walked, singled, and singled. Cubs manager, Jim Marshall—

no dummy himself—decided once through the batting order was enough and sent the big guy to the showers having achieved one measly out for his efforts. The Pirates would finish the first inning having sent fourteen batters to the plate while collecting eight hits, drawing three bases on balls, and scoring nine runs—eight more than they would need that afternoon.

The Cubs immediately answered in the bottom half of the inning the same way they would answer in the bottom half of every inning: no runs.

In the third inning, Pirates second baseman, Rennie Stennett (get used to hearing his name), singled and scored on a home run by Richie Hebner. It was now Pirates 11, Cubs 0.

In the fourth, Pirates hitters were tired from all that swinging, so Cubs pitcher Tom Dettore—always accommodating—hit a batter and walked another helping the visitors plate their twelfth run without need of a hit.

Then came the fifth. Stennett led off with his fourth hit, a double, which was followed by an error and two singles to score a pair of runs. Marshall, hoping to keep this one close, decided it was time to take out Dettore and replace him with his bullpen ace Oscar Zamora. The first batter, hulking Dave Parker, selected one of Oscar's dazzling pitches and deposited it approximately two miles away from home plate. When the ball finally landed, it was declared a home run, adding three more runs to the Pirates' total. The visitors banged out three more hits that inning adding another run and making the score eighteen-zip.

But you can never be too sure in this crazy game of baseball, so the Pirates scored a pair of runs in the sixth, and added two more in the seventh to close out the scoring and assure that even if the Cubs rallied to score three late touchdowns, they would still need a two-point conversion to tie.

His team may have had enough of pounding the locals, but Stennett—the little showoff—hadn't. Coming up in the eighth, he needed one more hit to become one of only a handful of players ever to collect seven hits in one game and he responded with a triple. Stennett finished the day no doubt pooped from all that swinging and running and scoring. He had gone seven-for-seven with a double, a triple, five runs scored, two runs batted in, and eleven total bases—numbers that were considerably better than those of the entire Cubs team that turned in a composite three-for-thirty, no extra base hits, no runs scored, no runs batted in, and three total bases.

Mercifully, the one-sided battle (22-0) had finally ended with beaten and battered Cubs players wailing in agony as they lay bleeding on Wrigley Field's lush, green carpet of grass.

Those hardy fans who managed to weather the storm and stick it out 'til the ugly end filed out of the ballpark dazed and confused. Whether or not this would end up being the last time any of these poor folks would find the courage to ever attend a Cubs game is impossible to know, but it would be difficult to blame any of them if the bloodshed they had just witnessed would have turned them on to other less dangerous, unpleasant forms of entertainment.

Perhaps Russian roulette.

Chapter 21: The Greatest Game Ever Played

Now that the previous chapter (*The Worst Game Ever Played*) has made you thoroughly sick, I feel it is my duty to try to make you feel better. Just think of me as a big bowl of chicken soup for your soul. Oh, who am I kidding? The only method that makes me feel better about the Cubs is bellying up to the bar and drinking my memory away. So think of me as a big bottle of Jack for your liver.

Anyway, despite our miserable century-long wait for a championship, we Cub fans have experienced a lot of great games—hell, you play 20,000 games in your history, there are bound to be some good ones in there somewhere. But which of those many contests is the greatest game ever played?

An old-timer would probably tell you the greatest game ever played in Cubs history was the famous "Homer-in-the-Gloamin'" game of 1938. He'd gaze off to the side and picture it in his mind as if it were unfolding again right before him. Then, he'd lean forward in his rocker, smile and tell you all about how with the score tied, darkness setting in, and the umpires ready to call the game, the grizzled old veteran Cubs player-manager, Gabby Hartnett, steps up to the plate and belts a home run with two outs in the bottom of the ninth to beat the Pirates and propel the Cubs to the World Series. There'd be tears in the old man's eyes as he relived the very same joy he felt all those years ago, and then he'd point a finger at you and insist that it was the most exciting moment in Cubs history. Finally, he'd fart real loud, fill his diaper, and take a nap.

Of course anyone who can remember that game is so old and blind he'd never be able to read this anyway, so screw him. That and the fact that I'm the author and therefore can decide whatever the hell I want to include in this book gives me the right to select the greatest game ever played. And believe me, the game I selected doesn't come from an era when grizzled old veterans named "Gabby" were playing baseball.

Instead, let's turn the pages back not quite so far to an era those of us still in control of our bodily functions can remember.

For Cub fans like me who had waded through years and years of crap waiting for our team to stop sucking and finish one stinking season in first place, the importance of this particular game played this particular year cannot be overstated. It is the game that will forever be known as "The Sandberg Game."

The date is June 23, 1984 and the team Cub fans love to hate — the Cardinals—are in town. Why do we hate the Cardinals so much? Because since our last trip to the World Series, they've played in ten of the damn things and won five of them—plus, they are rapists and pillagers. I made that part up.

It's a beautiful Saturday afternoon at Wrigley Field and this matchup between the longtime rivals is to be televised to a national audience on NBC. It's one of those rare years for the Cubs—they're good—and so the ballpark is overflowing with excited fans.

Leading 9-3 heading to the bottom of the sixth inning, the Cardinals appear on their way to an easy victory when the Cubs bust loose for five runs. Included in the rally is a two-run single (his third hit of the day) by budding Cubs star second baseman Ryne Sandberg.

St. Louis holds onto the one-run lead as the Cubs come up in the ninth. It looks rather bleak for the home team as Cardinals relief ace (and ex-Cub) Bruce Sutter, armed with his frightening split-finger fastball, takes the mound to face Sandberg leading off the inning. Unafraid, Ryno deposits one of Sutter's offerings into the left field bleachers. The game is tied and Cub fans go wild.

Despite Sandberg's heroics, the Cardinals respond with two runs in the top of the tenth to lead again by an 11-9 score. This time, Sutter gets two quick outs in the bottom half of the inning and it appears the rapists and pillagers will escape with a win. But not so fast! Bob Dernier draws a walk bringing to the plate the man who tied it up in the ninth. And again Sandberg delivers, powering his second home run in two innings off the supposedly unhittable Sutter. For the second time, bedlam visits Wrigley Field.

The Cardinals go scoreless in the top half of the twelfth setting the stage for more Cub heroics—this time from a very unlikely source. Leon Durham draws a leadoff walk, promptly steals second and advances on an errant throw—yes, we have pillagers too! The next two Cub batters are walked intentionally bringing to the plate light-hitting reserve infielder Dave Owen who looks barely strong enough to hold a bat. With the infield pulled in, Owen slaps a single scoring the winning run and sending Cub fans into wild merriment. The hated Cardinals are vanquished.

The thrilling comeback victory propels the Cubs onward to their first pennant of any kind in thirty-nine years and establishes Sandberg, who finishes the day with five hits and seven runs-batted-in, as much more than a budding star. He would go on to win the league's 1984 MVP award and eventually earn induction into the Hall of Fame.

So old-timer, it's true there may not have been any gloamin' in my choice for the greatest game ever played, but there certainly was some dramatic homerin'—two to be exact—one in the ninth and one in the tenth!

Get back to me when Gabby does that.

Chapter 22: Fifty Since Sixty

Watching the Cubs for half a century has pretty much turned my brain to mush, but it has also allowed me to see hundreds and hundreds (feels like millions) of Cubs players. From that huge collection of men who have worn Cubbie blue, I have selected my fifty favorite players since 1960. Most of the names on this list are there because they were good players, but some appear simply because, for whatever reason, I liked them, and this is my list so I can put anyone on it I want. If you have a problem with any of my choices, make your own damn list!

1. Ernie Banks – Shortstop/First Baseman (1953-1971)

"Mr. Cub" should be at the top of every baby boomer Cub fan's list. If he's not at the top of your list, you are an idiot. Note: If he *is* at the top of your list, you may still be an idiot, but for other reasons.

2. Billy Williams – Outfielder (1959-1974)

Billy had one of the sweetest swings ever swung which produced some of the hardest hits ever hit, making this sentence one of the coolest writes ever written.

3. Ron Santo – Third Baseman (1960-1973)

It took way too long, but Hall of Fame voters finally figured out that Santo belonged there. It sure would have been nice if they'd done it while Ronnie was still alive, but that would have required fewer Hall of Fame voters who are pricks.

4. Ryne Sandberg – Second Baseman (1982-1994, 1996-1997)

Now hear this, Joe Morgan: Ryne Sandberg was better than you! A great pure athlete, there wasn't anything the 1984 National League MVP couldn't do on the baseball field. Nine straight Gold Gloves at second base, a league-leading forty home runs in 1990, and fifty-four stolen bases in 1985 bear that out. And, unlike Morgan, he never felt the need to tell the world he was good.

5. Ferguson Jenkins – Pitcher (1966-1973, 1982-1983)

Six straight twenty win seasons pretty much says it all about this guy. Every fourth day, Jenkins was there on the mound, ready to go nine innings and in 1971 he did just that thirty times! That's twenty-nine more complete games than the entire Cubs pitching staff had in 2010. I guess Jenkins wasn't on a pitch count.

6. Sammy Sosa – Outfielder (1992-2004)

Sammy's hitting exploits may have been attained with the aid of chemicals and cork, but any Cub fan who says he or she wasn't turned on every time Sosa blasted one into orbit is a liar. You can't stand and cheer the man's exploits and then pretend you never did.

7. Andre Dawson – Outfielder (1987-1992)

Long before Kerry Wood pulled him out of the vines, "The Hawk" could do everything there is to do on a baseball diamond and did a lot of it on bad knees. As a free agent anxious to escape Montreal and play in a *real* baseball town, Dawson handed Dallas Green a blank check and said he'd sign for whatever amount Green selected. He was a great player, but a lousy negotiator.

8. Greg Maddux – Pitcher (1986-1992, 2004-2006)

Maddux, who looks more like a computer nerd than an athlete, holds the record for consecutive seasons (17) with fifteen or more wins. Too bad eleven of those seasons came in a Braves uniform, thanks to then-Cubs GM Larry Himes, who screwed up the works and let Maddux get away. Thanks Larry.

9. Mark Grace – First Baseman (1988-2000)

A fan favorite, Grace was one of the best pure hitters the Cubs have ever had as well as a good defensive first baseman. But his greatest contribution to baseball was his revelation on a television talk show of a little known strategy he called the "slumpbuster" where a struggling ballplayer lays the wood to the fattest, ugliest woman he can find. That, my friends, is desperation.

10.   Bill Buckner – First Baseman (1977-1984)

This guy played his guts out every moment he was on the field, and did it on a pair of bad ankles to boot. But he'll always be remembered for his error in game six of the 1986 World Series that won the game for the Mets. The good news is his misfortune can be blamed on The Curse of the Bambino and not on that stupid goat.

11.   Glenn Beckert – Second Baseman (1965-1973)

Beckert was Leo Durocher's favorite player on those good Cubs teams of the late '60s/early '70s, and the reason Leo liked him so much is because he made the most of mediocre talent by mastering the fundamentals. If Beckert were around today, he'd never make it to the majors because nobody gives a crap about fundamentals anymore.

12.   Don Kessinger – Shortstop (1964-1975)

A very good college basketball player at the University of Mississippi, Kessinger was a good-field, no-hit shortstop when he came up to the Cubs. After teaching himself to switch hit, he became a decent leadoff man for the Cubs, but his real strength was his outstanding ability to go deep in the hole, pirouette (French for "pirouette"), and throw a strike to first base.

13.   Rick Sutcliffe – Pitcher (1984-1991)

After coming over in June of '84 from the Indians, "The Red Barron" went on to win the National League's Cy Young award and lead the Cubs to their first divisional pennant. He was also one big dude who could hit the ball a mile when he connected.

14.   Jose Cardenal – Outfielder (1972-1977)

He couldn't have weighed more than 140 pounds, but Cardenal had surprising power to go with outstanding speed. The outfielder is also believed to be the only player ever to sit out a game because crickets kept him awake the night before.

15.   Kenny Holtzman – Pitcher (1965-1971, 1978-1979)

This lefty possessed one of the best arms in Cubs history—all he did was pitch no-hitters in '69 and '71. But he and manager Leo Durocher could never get along, so Holtzman was traded away to Oakland where he played on three straight world championship teams. So I guess it worked out pretty well for him.

16. Kerry Wood – Pitcher (1998, 2000-2008, 2011-2012)

His twenty strikeout performance as a rookie and his domination of the Braves in the 2003 Division Series were just flashes of what could have been. But a million injuries, ranging from a torn elbow ligament requiring Tommy John surgery to something as stupid as falling out of a hot tub, cut short a possible Hall of Fame career.

17. Derrek Lee – First Baseman (2004-2010)

After being part of the 2003 Marlins team that makes me want to puke every time I think of them, Lee came to the Cubs and became one of my favorites. Quite an accomplishment, what with the whole "being part of the 2003 Marlins team that makes me want to puke every time I think of them" thing.

18. Carlos Zambrano – Pitcher (2001-2011)

One of the most successful pitchers in Cubs history, Zambrano was a head case and an enemy to anyone (opposing players, teammates, umpires) or anything (water coolers, Gatorade dispensers, baseball bats) that got in his way, including himself.

19. Randy Hundley – Catcher (1966-1973, 1976-1977)

He holds the record for games caught in a single season—an incredible 160. Fans loved him because he played the game all out with guts and grit, but severe knee injuries cut his career far too short. Despite spawning Todd Hundley, fans *still* love Randy.

20. Shawon Dunston – Shortstop (1985-1995, 1997)

Dunston never saw a pitch he didn't like and so he swung at all of them. Hustling and aggressive, he had a flame-thrower of an arm at shortstop, which made first baseman Mark Grace earn his big salary.

21. Bill Hands – Pitcher (1966-1972)

A gutsy pitcher who would go out and keep the Cubs in every game he pitched whether he had his good stuff or not, Hands won twenty games in '69. Good thing he could pitch, because he was easily one of the worst hitters of all time.

22. Rick Reuschel – Pitcher (1972-1981, 1983-1984)

For a guy who made Don Zimmer look buff, Reuschel was an amazingly agile and complete athlete. A twenty game winner in '77, he was also an excellent fielder and decent hitter. And he looked just fabulous in those stretchy old powder blue pin-striped Cub uniforms of the late '70s.

23. Jim Hickman – Outfielder/First Baseman (1968-1973)

For two seasons ('69 and '70), Hickman was undoubtedly one of the greatest clutch hitters in Cubs history. He was particularly amazing in the late innings and both years almost single-handedly kept the Cubs in contention. Despite his heroics, Hickman was a painfully modest guy who quietly went about his job expecting nothing in return—just like today's ballplayers.

24. Lee Smith – Pitcher (1980-1987)

At 6'5", Smith was an intimidating sight to batters as he unleashed his blazing fastball. His total of 180 saves ranks him first among Cubs pitchers in that category. It's a shame he'll always be remembered for giving up that game-winning home run hit by nauseating Steve Garvey in game four of the 1984 NLCS.

25. Ryan Dempster – Pitcher (2004-present)

Picked up off the scrapheap by the Cubs when his once-promising career appeared to be over, Dempster gave the Cubs three solid seasons as a closer before switching to the starting rotation in '08. The Canadian-born Dempster is also the greatest hockey player the Cubs have ever had, which, I guess, is pretty meaningless since the Cubs are a baseball team.

26. Bill Madlock – Third Baseman (1974-1976)

In just three seasons with the Cubs, Madlock won two batting titles and then had the nerve to ask for big money. Phil Wrigley stubbornly refused to give Madlock what he wanted and traded him away prior to the '77 season. Wrigley died just one week after the season began while Madlock went on to a career that would feature two more batting titles and a World Series championship. Guess Madlock came out ahead in that one.

27. Leon Durham – Outfielder/First Baseman (1981-1988)

A bundle of super talent, "The Bull" was faster than a speeding bullet and more powerful than a locomotive, but Gatorade was his kryptonite.

28. Rick Monday – Outfielder (1972-1976)

Monday, a good centerfielder with power and decent speed, was a surprisingly effective lead-off man. But, he's best remembered for grabbing the American flag away from a couple of knuckleheads preparing to burn it in the outfield during a game at Dodger Stadium.

29. Keith Moreland – Catcher/Outfielder/First Baseman/Third Baseman (1982-1987)

Built like a brick shithouse, Moreland was surprisingly versatile for a guy who began his career as a catcher. He was moved to right field, played some first base, and even gave third base a shot. Moreland was never known for his defense, but the man could hit and played the game like he was still playing football at the University of Texas.

30. Jody Davis – Catcher (1981-1988)

Whenever Harry Caray would sing "Jody, Jody Davis, catcher without a fear" to the tune of the *Ballad of Davy Crockett*, it was a clear sign that Harry had reached his Budweiser limit for the day.

31. Gary Matthews – Outfielder (1984-1987)

"The Sarge" was the leader of the '84 Cub team that nearly made it to the World Series. His all-out hustle, clutch bat, and exciting defense (as in every catch was an adventure) made him a fan favorite.

32. Michael Barrett – Catcher (2004-2007)

He punched A. J. Pierzynski in the mouth. Enough said.

33. Willie Smith – Outfielder/First Baseman (1968-1970)

"Wonderful Willie" hit the dramatic game-winning home run on opening day 1969. But my favorite memory of Smith came in a game I attended. Smith was playing left field when one of the Bleacher Bums standing on the wall lost his balance and tumbled down feet first onto the field. Willie motioned the startled fan over, and meshing his fingers together, provided a boost for the bum to return up the vines and back into the bleachers. He saved the idiot a fine and appealed to my fondness for those who aid and abet lawbreakers.

34. Dave Kingman – Outfielder (1978-1980)

By all accounts, Kingman was a prick, but I don't care because for three seasons, the big leftfielder hit some of the longest home runs ever hit by a Cub not named Sosa.

35. Milt Pappas – Pitcher (1970-1973)

Pappas was one strike away from a perfect game when big, fat-ass plate umpire Bruce Froemming called balls on three consecutive close pitches. Despite the walk, Pappas got the next hitter to pop up to preserve the no-hitter. In one of the oddest celebrations in baseball history, Pappas was surrounded by joyous teammates as he angrily hollered expletives at Froemming.

36. Adolfo Phillips – Outfielder (1966-1969)

Phillips had tons of talent with blazing speed, strong defensive skills, and big-time power. But he could never quite put it all together and ended up in Durocher's doghouse, which led to Phillips' eventual exile to that baseball hell otherwise known as Montreal.

37. Moises Alou – Outfielder (2002-2004)

Urine good hands with Moises. It was revealed during Alou's Cubs career that he peed on his hands to toughen them up so he could get a good grip on the bat. If only Bartman had been in the john pissing on *his* hands during the eighth inning of game six of the 2003 NLCS.

38.   Joe Pepitone – Outfielder/First Baseman (1970-1973)

This guy was as goofy as they come, but he could hit and he played a great first base. In addition to baseball, Pepitone fancied himself a singer, loved the ladies, and had a number of different hairpieces to cover his bald spot.

39.   George Altman – Outfielder (1959-1962, 1965-1967)

Altman had a couple of great years for the Cubs in an otherwise so-so big league career. But the big left-handed hitter went on to have a long and successful "besuboru" career over in Japan where he smashed 205 home runs in seven years before saying, "Sayonara."

40.   Jerry Morales – Outfielder (1974-1977, 1981-1983)

The Cubs have had few better clutch hitters than Morales who drove in a lot of runs despite mediocre power. They've also had few better multi-taskers. He was once caught on camera unwrapping a piece of chewing gum and popping it into his mouth while circling under a fly ball.

41.   Larry Jackson – Pitcher (1963-1966)

A pretty good pitcher throughout his career, Jackson had one incredible year with the Cubs in '64 when he led the major leagues with 24 wins. But his greatest contribution to the Cubs was being part of the trade that brought Ferguson Jenkins to Chicago.

42.   Dick Ellsworth – Pitcher (1958, 1960-1966)

You wouldn't know it looking at his career numbers, but Ellsworth was actually a pretty decent lefty. He had one spectacular year ('63) in which he won twenty-two games with a 2.10 ERA, but his greatest performance as a Cub didn't even count. It came in an exhibition game against the White Sox when at the age of eighteen Ellsworth tossed a four-hit shutout. To Cub fans, that counts for something.

43.   Reed Johnson – Outfielder (2008-2009, 2011-present)

Johnson made the greatest diving catch I ever saw in a 2008 game in Washington. Playing centerfield, he ran full speed into left center, dove and miraculously snagged the ball before smashing his head into the wall with such impact that the downward curve in the bill of his cap was reversed upward. Amazingly, Johnson ran off the field without serious injury. It's that kind of effort that has made him one of my favorites.

44.   Joe Girardi – Catcher (1989-1992, 2000-2002)

Girardi was popular because he did all the little things that help a team win ballgames. And he was definitely a winner—after leaving the Cubs, of course—having caught in three World Series with the Yankees and managing them to the 2008 world championship.

45.   Glenallen Hill – Outfielder (1993-1994, 1998-2000)

I have to include on my list the only man ever to hit a homer that landed atop one of the rooftops on Waveland Avenue.

46.   Manny Trillo – Second Baseman (1975-1978, 1986-1988)

Few second basemen could turn a double-play as well as Manny. In addition, he was a pretty decent hitter and very good in the clutch. Like so many other Cubs, Manny had to be traded away to get to play in a World Series and was part of the 1980 Phillies ball club that won it all.

47.   Aramis Ramirez – Third Baseman (2004-2011)

By the time his Cubs career was nearing an end, Ramirez was playing third base like Ron Santo… if Santo had played third base *after* he'd lost both legs. But Aramis could sure hit the piss out of the ball, ranking sixth on the Cubs' all-time home run list.

48.   Joe Wallis – Outfielder (1975-1978)

"Tarzan" wasn't terribly good, but he was a lot of fun to watch. A daredevil who liked to dive into swimming pools from hotel roofs, Wallis was sometimes as reckless on the field once attempting a behind-the-back catch in a spring training game.

49.   Don Landrum – Outfielder (1962-1965)

A lousy hitter, Landrum was one of my early favorites—obviously my standards were pretty low back then. He earned a spot in my heart after making an athletic sliding catch in centerfield one afternoon. That play inspired me to try to copy it over and over and over again on the kitchen floor, which in turn inspired my mom to yell at me over and over and over again.

50.   Mick Kelleher – Infielder (1976-1980)

Mick wasn't much of a hitter, in fact he was an awful hitter, but he was a good little infielder and he hustled and played hard all the time, so he earns the last slot on this list. I also put him here because he and I have something in common: we hit the same number of career home runs.

Chapter 23: Enemies List

You wouldn't know it from some of the things I've written, but I'm really a pretty nice guy. I can't say that I've ever met a person I disliked to the point of hatred. Sure, there are plenty of people who annoy the hell out of me and I could do without them, but I feel no real hatred towards any of them. I am however capable of hating people I've never met (celebrities, politicians, and athletes) and I assure you I have never met any of the individuals on this list. My hatred for them is based purely within the context of baseball and the Cubs.

So taking a page from President Nixon—another guy I never met but hated with a passion—I give you my enemies list.

Tom Seaver

I hate this guy. Any Cub fan who survived the '69 season came away from it hating the entire New York Mets team, and especially Seaver. His smart-ass comments about the Cubs, and particularly Ron Santo, during that season immediately earned him a spot on this list. He later clinched numero uno on the list when he became a member of the White Sox.

Tony LaRussa

I hate this guy too. There are numerous reasons to hate LaRussa. First off, he managed both the White Sox and the Cardinals—yuck! Secondly, he has been called a genius for so long that he actually believes it and therefore acts like an arrogant prick. But he's had a good teacher. He's a close friend of Bobby Knight—the supreme king of all arrogant pricks.

Steve Garvey

All the years he played for the Dodgers, Garvey was a tough guy to like. He was too perfect with his muscular build and nice hair and all-American boy image, and his uniform was always nice and white and perfectly tailored. He was really kind of nauseating. And then as a member of the Padres he hit the game-winning home run in game four of the '84 NLCS to beat the Cubs and the nausea turned to all out hatred.

Hawk Harrelson

The White Sox announcer is clearly as jealous of the Cubs as all the Sox fans he broadcasts to. During interleague games between the Cubs and Sox, you can hear the absolute pain in his voice whenever the Cubs win and he really struggles to ever say anything nice about any of the Cubs players. Meanwhile, Cubs announcers always manage to say nice things—no matter how unappetizing that may be—about the White Sox. You can put it on the board that I look forward to the day he's told to go grab some bench because he gone from the broadcast booth. Yes!

Bruce Froemming

Yes I know, umpires are just doing their jobs, but Froemming was really bad at just doing his job for a long, long time. Towards the end of his career he was so fat he could barely bend over, which is kind of important if you're calling balls and strikes, but even in his younger, less fat, days he sucked. Froemming always seemed to be at his suckiest whenever the Cubs were involved. He screwed Milt Pappas out of a perfect game and nearly screwed the Cubs in game five of the 2003 Division Series.

A.J. Pierzynski

I'm not alone here—a recent poll of big leaguers revealed Pierzynski is the most hated player in major league baseball. If you are a Cub fan and you didn't absolutely love it when Michael Barrett belted him in the mouth, there's something wrong with you.

Jack McKeon

Sorry, but I'm one guy who wasn't feeling all warm and fuzzy about the old fart winning a World Series in 2003. McKeon has twice been the beneficiary of Cubs misfortune—as general manager of the San Diego Padres in '84 and as manager of the Florida Marlins in '03. Now that he's in his eighties I'm pretty sure he won't be coming back to hurt us anymore. But I won't rest easy until someone drives a stake through his heart.

Marty Brennaman

Old Triangle Head—the voice of the Cincinnati Reds—bashed Cub fans in 2008 calling us "far and away the most obnoxious fans in baseball." He went on to say that for that reason he roots against the Cubs. But the main reason to hate Marty is for giving the world his son Thom, whose grating and annoying voice is the reason your TV remote has a mute button.

Al Hrabosky

The "Mad Hungarian" specialized in acting like a jag-off whenever he came into a game in relief for St. Louis. His routine of turning his back to the batter, storming off the mound, and pounding his fist into his glove prior to every pitch may have excited mindless Cardinals fans (I know, redundant), but to the rest of us it was nothing more than a tired display of masturbation.

Joe Morgan

I just don't like this guy. Morgan was a terrific ballplayer who put together some outstanding years with the Reds during the "Big Red Machine" years. He had great speed and surprising power and was a good defensive second baseman. I have no problem recognizing that he was *one* of the top second basemen of all time. Morgan, however, seems to think he was *the* greatest of all time, and has always implied that Ryne Sandberg was not as good as he. Besides that, he's an annoying baseball analyst who over-analyzes every single thing that happens on the field.

Mike Schmidt

Five years after he bawled like a blubbering little girl at his retirement announcement, the former Phillies third baseman was inducted into the Hall of Fame. Then, as a member of the Hall's veterans committee, he always submitted a blank ballot believing players who weren't already voted in didn't deserve to ever get there. It's because of voters like Mike Schmidt that Ron Santo didn't win induction until after the veterans committee was dismantled and replaced by a new committee made up of members who actually voted. By then Ron was dead.

Ozzie Guillen

He's an idiot.

Part Four: Heading For Home

Modern Times

If you like the idea of a hot ball girl, an obscenity-filled tirade from an irate manager, and an obnoxious prick getting punched in the mouth, you'll love this section. But tread lightly! Heartbreaking losses, a clueless general manager, broken pitchers, and a fan who just couldn't keep his little hands to himself may make you hate this section as well.

Chapter 24: Lee Elia Goes Mother[lovin'] Nuts

With roughly a half-century under my belt as a Cub fan, I've seen thousands of games and in the process uttered thousands of expletives while throwing thousands of beer bottles at my TV screen. And that's on good days.

But whether the Cubs win or lose, my life doesn't change. I still have to get up each day and go to work, and pay my bills, and maintain a secret identity as I outrun the feds. The Cubs are merely a diversion—sometimes one that makes me crazy. The Cubs can frustrate the hell out of a fan like me, but imagine what it must be like for someone whose livelihood depends on the team's success—like the manager of the team.

The afternoon of April 29, 1983, the Cubs were roundly booed by fans while suffering a tough loss to the Dodgers at Wrigley Field. Following the game, Cub manager Lee Elia couldn't take any more and let loose with one of the greatest tirade's in baseball history—all of it caught on audio tape by a reporter.

Here for your enjoyment is a transcript of Elia's x-rated one man show. As a service to you, I have replaced the dirty words with nice words to protect you from whatever the fuck it is that offends people like you.

> I'll tell you one [lovin'] thing, I hope we get [lovin'] hotter than [sugar], just to stuff it up them 3,000 [lovin'] people that show up every [lovin'] day. Because if they're the real Chicago [lovin'] fans, they can kiss my [lovin'] [shapely bottom] right downtown, and PRINT IT!
>
> They're really, really behind you around here ... my [lovin'] [shapely bottom]. What the ... what the [love] am I supposed to do, go out there and let my [lovin'] players get destroyed every day and be quiet about it? For the [lovin'] nickel-dime people that show up? The mother[lovers] don't even work. That's why they're out

at the [lovin'] game. They oughta go out and get a [lovin'] job and find out what it's like to go out and earn a [lovin'] living.

Eighty-five percent of the [lovin'] world's working. The other fifteen come out here. It's a [lovin'] playground for the [popsicle]suckers. Rip them mother[lovers] ... rip them [lovin'] [popsicle]suckers like the [lovin'] players. We got guys bustin' their [lovin'] [shapely bottoms], and them [lovin'] people boo. And that's the Cubs? My [lovin'] [shapely bottom]. They talk about the great [lovin'] support that the players get around here. I haven't seen it this [lovin'] year....

The name of the game is hit the ball, catch the ball, and get the [lovin'] job done. Right now, we have more losses than we have wins. The [lovin'] changes that have happened in the Cub organization are multi-fold. All right, they don't show because we're five and fourteen. And ... unfortunately, that's the criteria of them dumb fifteen mother[lovin'] percent that come out to day baseball. The other eighty-five percent are earning a living.

It'll take more than a five and thirteen or five and fourteen to destroy the makeup of this club. ... I guarantee you that. There's some [lovin'] pros out there that wanna [lovin'] play this game. But you're stuck in the [lovin'] stigma of the [lovin'] Dodgers and the Phillies and the Cardinals and all that cheap [sugar].

All these mother[lovin'] editorials about Cey and [lovin'] ... ah ... the Phillie-itis and all that [sugar], it's... it's sickening. It's unbelievable. It really is. It's a disheartening [lovin'] situation we're in right now. Five and fouteen doesn't negate all that work.

We got 143 [lovin'] games left. What I'm tryin' to say is don't rip them [lovin'] guys out there. Rip me! If you wanna rip somebody, rip my [lovin'] [shapely bottom], but don't rip them [lovin'] guys, 'cause they're givin' everything they can give.

And once we hit that [lovin'] groove, it'll flow. And it will flow, the talent's there. I don't know how to make it any clearer to you. I'm frustrated, I ...I'll guarantee I'm frustrated. It'd be different if I walked into this room every day at 8:30 and saw a bunch of guys that didn't give a [sugar]. They give a [sugar]. And it's a tough National League East. It's a tough National League, period."

Yes, it appears something was bothering poor Lee that day.

But it wasn't long before he was put out of his misery as the Cubs fired him at mid-season and he found himself standing in the unemployment line with the other "dumb fifteen mother[lovin']] percent" without a job.

For the record, here are the final statistics:

[love]: 1

[lovin']: 34

Mother[lovin']: 2

Mother[lovers]: 2

[popsicle]suckers: 2

[shapely bottom(s)]: 5

[sugar]: 5

Total Expletives: 51

Chapter 25: They Rip My Heart Out

*W*hen I think back to 1984, my first thoughts are...

Boy, those were the good old days when I could drink beer all night and go to bed and sleep without having to get up to pee every couple of hours!

My next thoughts are of the Cubs and how after thirty-nine years of futility, they finally finished in first place winning the National League's Eastern Division pennant. Then I remember how the season ended—how everything turned to crap—and I get depressed and go to the fridge and grab a few beers. Finally, I go to bed and get up every couple of hours to pee, and well... it's just one vicious cycle.

That's why I try not to think about 1984 (or *Animal Farm*, or any other Orwell books) and just try to think about today. Nevertheless, it's my job to educate and inform my readers about the Cubs, so I will go to the fridge, grab a brewski, and take a somewhat happy, but mostly painful trip down memory lane.

First, the happy part...

On September 24, Rick Sutcliffe hurls a complete game as the Cubs clinch the National League's Eastern Division pennant in Pittsburgh. Cub fans everywhere jump up and down and Wrigleyville is packed with elated fans as they celebrate in front of Wrigley Field while the marquee proudly announces CUBS WIN!!! We can't believe what we've just seen—the Cubbies have won a pennant for the first time since a whole lot of people had died! We just can't wait for the regular season to end and the post-season to begin.

Now for the painful part...

The Cubs will be playing the San Diego Padres (literal translation: The Saint James Fathers)—a former expansion team with almost no history and ugly brown uniforms that make the players look like a bunch of turds. The Cubs, with lots of history and nice uniforms, are expected to trample the turds, scrape them from their cleats, and move on to the World Series.

Before the series even begins the Cubs get screwed. Because there are no lights at Wrigley Field and ABC—the big crybabies—demands prime time coverage of its weekend games, the series is changed to open in Chicago rather than San Diego. This means instead of having three home games, the Cubs will host just two. Already, the turds have an undeserved advantage.

Meanwhile, Chicago Tribune columnist, Mike Royko, writes an article prior to the series in which he calls people from San Diego "wimps," "quiche-eaters," and "surfers"—which, of course, they are. The article pisses off a lot of the wimps, quiche-eaters, and surfers and when the series switches to San Diego for game three, irate wimps, quiche-eaters, and surfers fill the ballpark and make lots of noise.

So here it is—a game-by-game rundown of the 1984 National League Championship Series.

Warning: You may want to have a cocktail or six ready to help numb the pain.

Game One

The series begins in a carnival-like atmosphere at Wrigley Field as the Cubs wipe up the turds 13-0 before a wild crowd of macho, pizza-eating, blue-collar workers. Bob Dernier leads off the bottom of the first with a home run and the Cubbies never look back. Pitcher Rick Sutcliffe cruises and adds a bomb of his own that lands on Sheffield Avenue. It's a great way to start the series.

One down, two to go!

Game Two

The Cubs go up two games to zip with a 4-2 win in front of another huge crowd of real Americans. Steve Trout pitches a strong game and Lee Smith comes on to earn the save as the Cubs leave Wrigley needing to win just one of three in San Diego.

JUST ONE MORE WIN!!

Game Three

Before an unusually loud gathering of wimpy, quiche-eating surfers, the Cubs take an early 1-0 lead in San Diego. Then the roof caves in and the Cubs fall 7-1. No reason to worry though, it's just a small setback.

Still, just one more win!

Game Four

This one is remembered by baseball historians as a classic game, but I remember it as a game that sucks. The Cubbies lead 3-2 heading to the bottom of the fifth, but the turds score a run in the fifth and with two in the seventh to take a 5-3 lead. Then Jody Davis belts a two-run homer to tie it in the eighth! But it's all just a setup so that we Cub fans can experience the pain of losing a heartbreaker. Nauseating pain-in-the-butt Steve Garvey homers with one on in the bottom of the ninth off Lee Smith to give the turds a 7-5 win. The series is now tied at two games apiece.

Just one more win...

Game Five

It looks like we're on our way to the World Series with a 3-0 lead heading to the bottom of the sixth and our best pitcher, Sutcliffe, on the mound. No way we can blow this one! Even after the turds score two in the sixth, we still have the lead. Only nine outs to go!

Then, all hell breaks loose. During the top half of the seventh inning, Gatorade is accidentally dumped on Leon Durham's glove. In the bottom of the seventh, the turds score four runs aided by a Durham error in which an easy ground ball escapes under his Gatorade-soaked glove. Another ball takes a bad hop over Ryne Sandberg's head and it's obvious the baseball gods hate us. The turds lead 6-3 and the stunned Cubs never come back.

Aw crap.

So they did it—ripped my heart right out of my chest. How could the Cubs lose out (again!) to a team they should have easily spanked? It was the '69 season all over again, except packed into one tiny five-game series. The Cubs were the better team and they lost to the San Diego Freakin' Padres—a former expansion team with no history and poop-colored uniforms for crying out loud!

The good news is the turds were flushed down the toilet four-games-to-one by Detroit in the World Series. That, and binge drinking, helped take a little bit of the sting away—but not much.

I could probably go on-and-on about how the Cubs losing this series ruined my life, but I'd better wrap it up. My beer wants out.

Chapter 26: The Belle of the Balls

*F*or years and years I would watch the Cubs kick the ball around on television with the gnawing feeling that something wasn't quite right. I couldn't quite put my finger on it, but I knew something essential was missing. I'd scan the TV screen trying to figure out what it was that was sorely lacking.

I would sit and think...

Well sure, we could use better players—that's a given. Our pitchers suck and, hell, I'd be happy if we had someone who could hit the damn ball out of the infield, for Christ's sake! But no, it's something less obvious than that. What is it? What is missing?

Then it hit me.

We need a hot chick! We don't have any hot chicks sitting down on the field. A hot chick would make watching these losers so much more enjoyable.

Apparently the Tribune Company was coming to the same conclusion because in 1982, they decided it was time they hired a hot chick to sit down on the field and they did just that. Her name was Marla Collins and she was given the official position of "ball girl."

The Cubs had always had people who would collect foul balls and bring a fresh set of baseballs to the home plate umpire. When I was a kid, it was ancient PA announcer Pat Peiper who would sit near the Cubs dugout and handle those duties, and later, batboys would do the same.

But now the Cubs had a chick—an out and out babe—handling those chores and I, like every other male Cub fan (and probably some of the ladies too), had a reason to keep watching even though our team was stinking up the joint.

The Tribsters—no dummies, at least not yet—made sure we men took notice of their new goods. They had her seated next to the visitor's dugout in an area that just happened to be in line of one of the camera angles. Collins was outfitted in a modified Cubs uniform tailored to accentuate her curves. She would wear long pants on cold days, but when the weather was warm she blessed us with very short shorts that showed off her perfectly shaped legs, the right one of which featured a small tattoo of a flower on the upper thigh. I never saw Pat Peiper's legs, but I'm pretty sure they never looked like that!

After years of watching big, ugly ballplayers spit tobacco and adjust their cups, seeing this sexy young woman right there on my TV, seemingly calling out my name, made watching the Cubs fun again. I wasn't sitting in my recliner wondering what was missing from my TV screen anymore. The picture was complete. I had the Cubs (for better or for awful) and I had Marla.

Cubs' broadcaster Harry Caray was particularly smitten with the young beauty and would mention her name in every broadcast. During one game in particular, on what apparently was the first day of the season cold enough for her to wear long pants, Harry told the fans, "Hey, we see Marla Collins without shorts for the first time." After a few moments, Harry realized what he had just said and pretty much laughed until he cried for the rest of the inning.

Cub fans and Harry weren't the only ones eyeing the ball girl. It wasn't long before Marla had drawn the attention of the good people at *Playboy* magazine who eventually managed to coax her into truly letting us see her without shorts for the first time. By the middle of the '86 season, word was out that Marla was to appear nude in the September issue.

The Tribune Company—not at all happy someone else was about to benefit from exploiting their hot commodity—decided it was time to pretend they were appalled by the idea of their ball girl being viewed as a sex object and fired her for "behavior unbecoming an employee." After four-and-a-half wonderful years, Marla was gone (tears streaming from my eyes). She was replaced with another girl, but it just wasn't the same and eventually, ownership did away with the whole ball girl idea completely.

For the record, I purchased that September copy of *Playboy* as soon as it came out and I assure you Marla did not disappoint. In fact, if she had been *my* employee, she would not have been fired but rather given a big raise for "behavior we encourage."

I still miss Marla and think of her often. At times I have watched games wishing she were there again to ease some of the pain. Especially now—as I write this the Cubs are about to lose their twelfth straight game and my interest in this latest collection of stumblebums is waning.

Marla, please save me!

Chapter 27: Mathematical Proof That Larry Himes is a Numbskull

As everyone knows by now, we have former Cubs general manager Larry Himes to thank for losing Hall of Fame pitcher Greg Maddux to the Atlanta Braves. This means that Himes saved us the pain and agony of watching Maddux win 194 games over the eleven year period of 1993 through 2003. What a burden that would have been! That works out to 17.6 wins per year for Maddux over that period. The way I figure it—and I *am* a math genius—the loss of Maddux cost the Cubs three first place finishes, which would have given us five trips to the post-season during those eleven years.

I hear what you're saying:

"Frank, how could you possibly know that? You can't assume that Maddux would have won the same number of games with the Cubs that he won with the Braves. You would have to take into consideration that he would have a different lineup of hitters supporting him and different fielders behind him. He would also have to face the Braves a couple of times a year and not face the Cubs, plus he would be pitching in a different ballpark, different weather conditions, etc. Besides, even if he did win the same number of games, he still would have been pitching every fifth day in the rotation, which means that someone in the Cubs' rotation would not have been there and that guy's win total would have to be subtracted from the Cubs' win total. So to be totally accurate, you would have to use a crazy, intricate formula devised by some mad genius that brings into consideration all of those factors."

My response to you is:

I already thought of all that, you smarty-pants! That's why I devised the following crazy, intricate formula:

Cubs Wins plus Maddux Wins minus Other Guy's Wins times Team Factor plus Ballpark Factor plus Weather Factor divided by pi equals Projected Cub Wins.

Now that's a mouthful, isn't it? So here is the formula written in an easy-to-understand equation:

$$(CW + MW - OGW) * (TF + BF + WF) / \pi = PCW$$

CW stands for Cubs Wins, MW is Maddux Wins, and OGW represents Other Guy's Wins. The "other guy" stands for the least effective Cubs starter during a given year who would certainly have been replaced by Maddux had he (Maddux) not been wearing the wrong uniform.

Team Factor (TF) comes from a complicated formula that includes team batting, team fielding, and bullpen statistics. Ballpark Factor (BF) is nearly as complicated and takes into consideration such factors as park dimensions, wall height, and grass thickness. With the help of world-renowned WGN Meteorologist Tom Skilling, the Weather Factor (WF) was devised using such variables as average temperature, humidity, dew point, and all kinds of other meteorological crap that goes way over my head (Thank you Tom!). The bottom line is that those formulas yielded the following numbers for 1993:

$$Team\ Factor = 2.0695$$

$$Ballpark\ Factor = .9613$$

$$Weather\ Factor = .1092$$

Please note that these numbers change from year-to-year based on team rosters, weather conditions such as "El Nino," and the fact that the Braves moved to a new ballpark in 1997.

The final key to my formula is the use of pi (π), which as any high school math student will tell you is, "A Greek letter that kind of looks like an anvil and for some reason represents the number 3.14159265∞."

We will round that number off to 3.14 in order to simplify our calculations. Why pi you may be asking? Well, for one thing, pi is really cool because you can just throw it into a formula and somehow get the right answer. I mean "pi r squared (πr^2)" gives you the area of a damn circle, for crying out loud! Nobody really understands how it works, it just does. Secondly, I believe that any mathematical formula should have pi in it somewhere. After all, the guy who invented pi didn't go through all that trouble just for the fun of it. He intended for us to use it in really complicated formulas. So I am using pi in my formula if for no other reason than as a tip of the hat to the pi guy.

[Author's note: By the way, the symbol ∞, which looks like an eight lying on its side, represents "infinity." This means that the value for π goes on forever! In other words, π is equal to 3.14159265358979323384526433832795028841971693993751058209749445923078164062820839862803482, etc., etc., etc., forever and ever, yadda, yadda, yadda, blah, blah, blah... Pretty scary stuff when you think about it, huh? I mean the pi guy came up with a number that never ends! Kind of like this author's note...]

No, this is not a perfect formula—I know it has some flaws—but it works for the theme of this chapter, which is **Larry Himes is a numbskull**. Below, I will show you, using my formula, how much better the Cubs would have been had Larry Himes listened to his mother and become an accountant.

Now I know that some of you are thinking that I'm being a bit rough on Himes—after all, he made the trade that brought Sammy Sosa to the Cubs. Yes it is true that Himes made the trade for Sammy, but I would call that just dumb luck. When that trade was made, Sosa was just a player with potential—he was not yet a star. Maddux, however, was indeed a star—the National League's Cy Young Award winner—and Himes just let him walk away, even though Maddux wanted to stay with the Cubs. I would call that just plain dumb.

So let's plug some numbers into my formula and see what we come up with. In 1993, the Cubs won 84 games, Greg Maddux won 20 games, and the Cubs' fifth starter, Frank Castillo, won five games. Here is the formula with all the numbers in place and the final results:

$$(84 + 20 - 5) * (2.0695 + .9613 + .1092) / 3.14 = 99$$

This means that the Cubs would have won 99 games in 1993, which would have been good enough for a first place finish in the

National League Eastern Division, two games ahead of the actual division winner, Philadelphia.

That wasn't so hard, was it? Now let's do the same thing with 1994. The Cubs won 49 games during that strike-shortened year. Maddux had sixteen wins and the Cubs number five starter, Kevin Foster, won just three games. Again, we plug the numbers into the formula and get the following results:

$$(49 + 16 - 3) * (2.0703 + .9613 + .1084) / 3.14 = 62$$

This time the Cubs would have won 62 games, which would have resulted in a third place finish in the National League's Central Division, just four games back of first place Cincinnati.

By now you're probably getting a little bored with doing the formula, so I have gone ahead and done it for you, covering the entire eleven year period during which Maddux was wearing the wrong uniform. Below is a table with the final results (Fig. 19.3). Please note the changes in the three factors (TF, BF, and WF) from year-to-year based on changing conditions. Again, those numbers come from very complicated formulas that, quite honestly, *I* don't even understand. Just trust me, my people tell me they are correct.

A couple of other clarifications: PCW = Projected Cub Wins; PF = Projected Finish; AF = Actual Finish.

Year	(CW	+ MW	− OGW)	* (TF	+ BF	+ WF)	/ π	PCW	PF	AF
1993	84	20	5	2.0695	.9613	.1092	3.14	99	1	4
1994	49	16	3	2.0703	.9613	.1084	3.14	62	3	5
1995	73	19	7	2.0692	.9613	.1095	3.14	85	1 tie	3
1996	76	15	5	2.0500	.9613	.1287	3.14	86	2	4
1997	68	19	6	2.0567	.9621	.1212	3.14	81	2	5
1998	90	18	7	2.0687	.9621	.1092	3.14	101	2 wc	2 wc
1999	67	19	2	2.0701	.9621	.1078	314	84	3	6
2000	65	19	3	2.0689	.9621	.1090	3.14	81	3	6
2001	88	17	9	2.0588	.9621	.1191	3.14	96	1	3
2002	67	16	1	2.0607	.9621	.1172	3.14	82	3	5
2003	88	16	8	2.0717	.9621	.1062	3.14	96	1	1
Totals	815	194	56	---	---	---	--	953	1.7	3.8

Fig. 19.3 – Table with the final results

Looking at the table, it is easy to see what an impact losing Maddux had on the success of the Cubs during his absence. Instead of just one first place finish and two post-season appearances, the Cubs would have won four division titles and one wild card spot resulting in five trips to the post-season. The loss of Maddux cost the Cubs 138 wins over that period (an average of nearly 13 wins per year) and meant an average finish of fourth place rather than second place.

I didn't make these numbers up folks—it's all right there! With an intricate formula that factored in numerous variables, we have proven that Larry Himes is indeed a numbskull.

Now if you'll excuse me, I'm going to go see what's in the fridge. All this talk about pi has made me hungry.

Chapter 28: Again They Rip My Heart Out

*T*his one hurts like hell. It hurts worse than '69 and '84 combined. The wounds are still a little too fresh. My wife says I should skip this one—write about something else.

"It's too soon," she says. "You'll get all upset, and then you'll be down and depressed again. Remember how long it took us to get you back to your happy place? Don't put me through that again. I beg of you, please! Please!!!"

Sorry Honey, but if I am going to write about being a Cub fan, I have to include *everything*—the good, the bad, and the Bartman. Besides, my therapist encourages me to talk about *all* the painful experiences in my life—you know, like the vasectomy you made me get. He says it's good for me to let things out.

So, I sit here at the keyboard trying to figure out how to write about this without going all Lee Elia on everybody. Because when I put myself back there, back to that night, back to that inning, back to that play, I just want to go into a tirade and start bleepin' this and bleepin' that. But, I can't do that. I must control myself and handle this like a professional. I must handle it like a man just relating a story to his readers. I must have a couple of drinks before I continue.

Be right back...

OK, that took a lot longer than expected. You know how just a couple drinks turns into waking up several hours later in a jail cell? Well anyway, I made bail and I'm back at the keyboard.

Before I get started, if you'll pardon me, I have a question for Commissioner Bud Selig. Hey Bud, why are the series that make up the first round of the post-season called "Division Series"? The Cubs and Braves aren't in the same division, so they're not playing for the championship of a division. The League Championship Series makes sense because the teams playing in it are from the same league, and the World Series makes sense because the teams playing in it are from the same world. But Division Series makes no sense. Oh, and one other question, Bud. What's that thing on the top of your head?

Now that I got that off my chest, here is a quick recap of the 2003 National League Division Series (stupid name) between the Chicago Cubs and the Atlanta Braves.

2003 National League Division Series (stupid name)

Game One

Turner Field in Atlanta is loaded with Cub fans because Braves fans don't really care unless it's the World Series—spoiled SOBs! The Cubs take game one of the Division Series 4-2 behind the strong pitching of Kerry Wood and run production from unlikely sources. Catcher Paul Bako—easily one of the worst hitters in baseball—drives in the first Cub run with a 2-out bases loaded walk and Wood follows with a 2-run double. Tomahawk chop this, Braves fans!

Game Two

Again Cub fans nearly outnumber Braves fans and are no-doubt excited when it looks like the Cubs are on their way after jumping on Braves pitcher Mike Hampton with two runs in the first. Sammy Sosa drives in both runs with a double that barely misses being a home run by inches. The Braves come back though to win 5-3. Now it's on to Chicago where the Cubs can win it with a pair of victories.

Game Three

It's a cool, overcast night at Wrigley, but it doesn't matter to Cub fans who pack the ballpark to see their Cubbies and Mark Prior. Prior's opponent is none other than ex-Cub, current Cub nemesis, and future Hall of Famer Greg Maddux. After the Cubs jump out to an early 2-0 lead in the first, the two pitchers trade goose-eggs until the eighth when the Braves finally score a run. But, the Cubs add a run in the bottom of the eighth and Prior sets the Braves down in the ninth to get the complete-game victory. A win in game four at Wrigley and the series is over!

Game Four

Cub fans are hoping to celebrate and it looks like we might when our heroes score a run in the third. But a pair of Chipper Jones home runs give the Braves a 6-2 lead heading to the bottom of the eighth. Eric Karros tries to single-handedly keep the Cubs in it with his second home run of the game making it 6-3 after eight innings. The Cubs rally for a run in the ninth and have the tying run at the plate with two outs when Sosa belts a fly ball to deep center to end the game. Damn! The Cubs will have to go back to Wrigley Field South and win it on the road.

Game Five

Turner Field is packed with Cub fans again. It's hard to believe fans of any team in post-season play would show as much disinterest as Braves fans have in this series. By the time this one ends, Cub fans are celebrating in the stands in Atlanta and on the streets of Chicago. Behind another dominant performance by Wood plus home runs by Alex Gonzalez and Aramis Ramirez, the Cubbies roll to a 5-1 win. The Cubs win their first post-season series in 95 years! Now it's time to give the Florida Marlins a whoopin'.

2003 National League Championship Series

So it's on to the National League Championship Series. The Cubs, by virtue of winning their division, have home-field advantage against a team called the—I'm not making this name up—Florida Marlins, who I believe are champions of the Florida State League. Cub fans are excited about our chances having knocked off the Braves without much trouble and now as a reward we get to play a minor league team!

Game One

As usual, Wrigley Field is overflowing with Cub fans. Are there any Marlins fans here? Not likely. Marlins fans rarely show up in Miami, let alone Chicago. (By the way, here's a rule that should be instituted immediately: If you do not draw at least two-million fans, you are ineligible for post-season play—case closed. Why should the rest of the world be stuck watching you if your own fans don't want to see you play?)

It's looking like this is going to be an easy one for the Cubs after we jump out to a 4-0 lead in the first inning. Florida bounces back however, and heading to the ninth, the game is tied 6-6. The Marlins score two in the top half to take the lead, but with two outs and a man on in the bottom of the ninth, Sosa hits a bomb onto Waveland Avenue and Wrigley Field is up for grabs. Unfortunately, Florida scores one in the eleventh and the Cubs lose a tough one by a 9-8 score.

Game Two

Apparently, the Cubs are determined to even the series because they come out and beat the crap out of the Marlins winning by a score of 12-3. The Cubs belt four home runs, including a Sosa shot that actually orbits the Earth once before hitting the roof of the camera shed below the scoreboard. Meanwhile, Prior is once again excellent as he goes seven strong innings for the win. With the series even at one, we head to that stupid-looking stadium in Florida.

Game Three

The stupid-looking stadium in Florida is filled for game three—must be half-price night for seniors. However, a good portion of the crowd (as usual) is made up of Cub fans.

Anyway, the Cubs win a thriller 5-4 with a run in the top of the eleventh to take a two-games-to one-lead. By winning, the Cubs have assured themselves of a trip home, if necessary.

Game Four

The Cubs bash Dontrelle Willis by a score of 8-3. Aramis Ramirez is the hitting star for the Cubs as he smashes two home runs including a grand slam. Willis, who couldn't find the plate if he used a GPS, walks five and gives up six runs in 2 2/3 innings. So now the Cubbies are up 3-1 in the series. The only question is where they will celebrate—Miami or Chicago.

Game Five

The Cubs lose 4-0, but no big deal. We have games six and seven in Chicago. World Series here we come!!!

Game Six

If the '84 NLCS is a mini version of the '69 season, this game is an itty-bitty version of the '84 NLCS. It hurts to even think about this game. We have it right in our hands! We have the damn game won! There's just no way we can lose this game. We have Prior on the mound in total control, mowing them down, and we have the lead, and we're down to just five more outs—just FIVE STINKIN' OUTS!—and...and...this slap hitter named Castillo is up and he... and he slaps a pop fly down the left field line and... uh... Alou is moving over into foul territory... and... well... I... I just can't do it... I can't relive it. I'm sorry, I just *cannot* do it.

If you're so damn nosy and just *have* to know what happened, look it up yourself! What? Do I have to do everything around here?

I need a beer.

Game Seven

I'm *way* too pissed to write about any of this crap. Just look it up yourself.

GAME SEVEN SUCKS!

Chapter 29: What if Bartman Had Gone Pee?

So what would have happened if Steve Bartman had had a lot to drink that night—maybe a couple of 32-ounce Cokes? Let's suppose Stevie had been holding it all through the game, but just couldn't hold it anymore and decided to finally go take a leak during the top half of the eighth inning. Suppose he was standing at one of those long troughs emptying his bladder at the time Luis Castillo lifted that pop foul that drifted past the Cubs bullpen. What would have happened if Moises Alou had caught that ball?

I know what you're saying: "But Frank, there is no way anyone could know the answer to that question. It is impossible to know what would have happened after the catch had been made. And what in the world is Bartman doing drinking a couple of 32-ounce Cokes anyway? Jeez, all that caffeine isn't healthy, is it?"

You make some good points, but thanks to this wonderful computerized world we live in, I have determined exactly what would have happened had Alou made the catch. Because of computerized baseball games, we are now able to replay games (or parts of games) and determine what *would* have happened if certain factors were introduced—like a full bladder.

Regarding the caffeine, we don't know for sure what Steve was drinking that night—he may have been doing shots of Jack—the point is, he apparently didn't have enough to drink because in the top of the eighth inning instead of standing at the urinal, he was sitting in his seat prepared to screw up the works and piss off Cub fans like myself who have the good sense to keep our stinking little hands to ourselves!

One of the companies that manufacture computerized baseball games is APBA. Now these computerized games are quite expensive and I don't have that kind of cash, so I had to settle for using the board version of their game. The APBA board game, which has been available for over fifty years, includes cards for each individual player and a pair of dice. Instead of a computer doing all the work, you simply roll the dice, get numbers from the player cards, match them to numbers on the boards, and end up with what might have been. It may sound a bit complicated, but it works. And it's kind of fun to play if you are a total loser and have no life.

Each year, APBA puts out a new set of cards based on the statistics of each player from the previous year. While the board game is not as expensive as the computerized version, it still requires a lot more bread than I have right now, so I had to get a little creative and make up my own cards. I still have the game that I bought forty years ago—when it was a lot cheaper, and I was a total loser without a life—and I still have the player cards from that year. Of course no one who played with the Cubs or the Marlins had a player card way back in 1972—in fact most of the guys hadn't even been born yet. So I went through the player cards I had and tried to match up as closely as I could the playing abilities of the players of '72 with the players of the Cubs and Marlins of '03.

After selecting cards for each of the players on the two teams, I made some minor adjustments to some of the cards. Obviously, it is unlikely that a card truly reflecting the abilities of Antonio Alfonseca, for instance, would be found in the '72 set. To the best of my knowledge there were no pitchers in the big leagues with six fingers at that time (If Three-Finger Brown had been around then, I could have used him twice.). So I did some tweaking here and there to get things just right.

I got lucky with Moises Alou because his dad, Felipe, who was similar to Moises as a hitter, was playing in the big leagues in '72. So I was able to use Felipe's card for Moises and just added some power to the numbers because son had more pop than his pop did.

Below are a three of the adjusted cards (Fig. Something—I've lost track of how many figures I've had so far), including that of Alou. Note that I used a Nolan Ryan card for Mark Prior and an Eliseo Rodriguez card for Ivan Rodriguez. Luckily, none of the cards required very many adjustments other than the names of the players.

Fig. Something - Adjusted APBA cards from 1972 (when I was a total loser without a life)

Using my adjusted cards, I resumed the game from the point at which Alou would have caught the foul ball by Castillo had Bartman been peeing like a good little boy.

Keep in mind that had the catch been made by Alou, everything would have changed. Momentum would have changed, strategy would have changed, and the mental outlook of the players would have changed. Not only that, but Steve would have returned to his seat a happy man because his bladder would have been empty and the Cubs would still have had the lead. Therefore, you will see changes in the results of the Marlins' at bats in the remainder of their half of the eighth as well as the ninth, plus changes in the results of the Cubs' at bats in the bottom of the eighth.

Below, with a tip of the cap to my good friends at Retrosheet.org, I have included the play-by-play from the actual game interspersed with the play-by-play from the APBA game. The APBA play-by-play is in **bold** print. Please make note of the differences.

MARLINS 8TH: Mordecai flied to left; Pierre doubled to left; Castillo walked while Pierre advanced to third on a wild pitch; Rodriguez singled to left [Pierre scored, Castillo to second]; Cabrera reached on an error by Gonzalez [Castillo to third, Rodriguez to second]; Lee doubled to left [Castillo scored, Rodriguez scored, Cabrera to third]; FARNSWORTH REPLACED PRIOR (PITCHING); Lowell was walked intentionally; Conine hit a sacrifice fly to right [Cabrera scored (unearned), Lee to third, Lowell to second]; HOLLANDSWORTH BATTED FOR FOX; Hollandsworth was walked intentionally; Mordecai doubled to left [Lee scored (unearned), Lowell scored (unearned, but earned for the pitcher), Hollandsworth scored (unearned, but earned for the pitcher)]; REMLINGER REPLACED FARNSWORTH (PITCHING); Pierre singled to right [Mordecai scored (unearned, but earned for the pitcher)]; Castillo popped to second; 8 R, 5 H, 1 E, 1 LOB. Marlins 8, Cubs 3.

MARLINS 8TH: Bartman went to take a leak; Mordecai flied to left; Pierre doubled to left; Castillo fouled out to left on a great catch by Alou; Rodriguez struck out. 0 R, 1 H, 0 E, 1 LOB. Marlins 0, Cubs 3.

CUBS 8TH: URBINA REPLACED HOLLANDSWORTH (PITCHING); Ramirez struck out; Karros flied to left; Gonzalez popped to second; 0 R, 0 H, 0 E, 0 LOB. Marlins 8, Cubs 3.

CUBS 8TH: BUMP REPLACED FOX (PITCHING); Bartman returned to his seat with an empty bladder and another 32-ounce Coke; Ramirez homered to left; Karros homered to left; Gonzalez popped to second; Bako grounded out to second; Prior homered to left; Lofton grounded to second; 3 R, 3 H, 0 E, 0 LOB. Marlins 0, Cubs 6.

MARLINS 9TH: ALFONSECA REPLACED GONZALEZ (PITCHING); MARTINEZ REPLACED REMLINGER (PLAYING SS); Rodriguez lined to center; Cabrera singled to left; Lee grounded into a double play (third to second to first) [Cabrera out at second]; 0 R, 1 H, 0 E, 0 LOB. Marlins 8, Cubs 3.

MARLINS 9TH: Cabrera struck out; Lee struck out; Lowell struck out; 0 R, 0 H, 0 E, 0 LOB. Marlins 0, Cubs 6.

CUBS 9TH: ENCARNACION REPLACED CABRERA (PLAYING RF); Bako was called out on strikes; Martinez flied to right; Lofton popped to third; 0 R, 0 H, 0 E, 0 LOB. Marlins 8, Cubs 3.

CUBS 9TH: Not necessary for the Cubs to bat in the ninth because they would have already won the game 6-0!

Do you see how different things would have been if Bartman had been in the potty instead of his seat? Energized by Alou's great catch, Prior comes back to strike out Ivan Rodriguez to end the eighth inning and preserve the Cubs' three-run lead. In the bottom of the eighth, Aramis Ramirez and Eric Karros hit back-to-back jacks and Prior (still energized) smashes one onto Waveland because instead of Ugueth Urbina, he is facing some guy named Nate Bump. Why Nate Bump, you ask? Because the computer chose him to pitch. Well not really the computer—I chose him to pitch—but had I been using the computerized version of the game, I'm sure it would have chosen him to pitch.

Then in the top of the ninth, with the crowd standing and roaring on every pitch, Prior, pitching on pure adrenalin, strikes out the side and the Cubs are headed to the World Freakin' Series!

So there it all is in black-and-white. If Steve had had a couple of 32-ouncers, or a six-pack of Old Style, or if he was really old and had bladder control problems, the Cubs would have won the damn game 6-0 and no one would even know his name.

I know I'm supposed to feel bad for Bartman, and I'm supposed to say it really wasn't his fault the Cubs lost, and I'm supposed to say if I had been sitting there, I would have tried to catch the ball too, and blah, blah, blah. But sometimes we need a scapegoat and my therapist tells me I *definitely* need one so that all my anger and frustration doesn't become pent up inside me and cause my blood pressure to rise to the point where I have a stroke or something. And then poor Steve would have *that* hanging over his head too. So Bartman, my man, I'm actually doing you a favor here.

Now if you'll pardon me, I have some work to do. Gotta dig through my APBA cards so we can see what would have happened in game five of the '84 NLCS if Gatorade had never been invented.

Chapter 30: We Don't Need No Stinkin' Pitch Counts!

Call me old school, but I hate pitch counts. I hate pitch counts and I'm tired of hearing about them. I miss the old days when a starting pitcher would pitch deep into ball games—maybe even pitch the whole damn thing, if you can imagine that—but those days are long gone.

We are raising a generation of pitchers who can't make it past the sixth inning without their poor little arms getting tired. There's a tremendous fear among owners, GMs, and managers of pitchers developing sore arms and so we have these damn pitch counts to make sure the poor babies are not overworked. But it's this coddling that has helped contribute to arm problems and it starts at the lowest levels. If a pitcher is only allowed to throw five innings in college and in the minor leagues, he will never be conditioned to go much further into a game at the major league level.

Pitchers arms are no longer conditioned to throw a lot of pitches, so now in order to win ballgames, you need a strong, deep bullpen. And you have guys in the bullpen who are accustomed to throwing only so many innings too. They throw every damn day now because the starters are out by the seventh inning, so you have seventh inning pitchers, eighth inning pitchers, and closers. And don't ever ask an eighth inning guy to pitch the seventh, or a closer to come into the game in the eighth and pitch more than one inning. Throws the poor bastards completely off their game.

And this all brings me to Kerry Wood and Mark Prior. It seems like centuries ago now, but as recently as 2003, those two gave the Cubs the best young pair of starting pitchers in baseball. But then injuries started piling up and the once dynamic duo weren't so dynamic anymore.

Wood's problems started several years before he and Prior were the dynamic duo. Following his rookie year of '98—a year in which he tied the major league record with twenty strikeouts in one game—Wood had to have "Tommy John surgery" to repair his sore right elbow. In case you're not familiar with it, Tommy John surgery is named after

Lou Gehrig who... wait a minute, I have my notes mixed up... hold on... here it is... Tommy John surgery is named after Tommy John who was the first pitcher to successfully return from said surgery and pitch effectively.

In spring training of 2004, it was Prior's turn—this time with an inflamed Achilles tendon, and a sore elbow, and a runny nose, and an endless assortment of maladies. Over the next few years, Wood and Prior would continue to make numerous trips to the disabled list only to come back, throw a few pitches, and break down again.

Of course all of this pitch count nonsense wouldn't be required if pitchers were trained from the outset to throw more pitches. One of the greatest eras for starting pitchers was the '60s. Think of the names: Sandy Koufax, Don Drysdale, Bob Gibson, Juan Marichal, Steve Carlton, Ferguson Jenkins. By the time they put on their first major league uniforms, pitchers of that era were built to last—they weren't so fragile. They were worked hard in the minors and arrived to the big leagues physically and mentally strong. These men were never on pitch counts—they were allowed to throw nine innings and their arms and minds became conditioned to handle a heavy workload. They started each game expecting to pitch nine innings and were disappointed if they failed.

Had they come along in the '60s, Wood and Prior probably would have terrorized batters for many years to come. But these aren't the '60s and instead they shattered into little pieces like so many young pitchers in today's baseball world do. That's just the way it is now and there's no turning back. Pitch counts—as much as I hate them—have become necessary.

Today you hear broadcasters refer to a pitcher who throws 200 innings in a season as a guy who "gives you a lot of innings." By today's standards that may be true, but in 1971 Ferguson Jenkins started 39 games for the Cubs, completed 30 of them, and pitched a total of 325 innings. Now that's a lot of innings! From 1967 through 1972, Jenkins started 234 games and completed 140 of them. He just went out there and threw the damn ball, and he was never hurt.

I recently called Jenkins and asked him about all the pitches he threw and all the innings he worked and if he thought he would have been better off with a pitch count. He laughed and replied, "Pitch count? I didn't need no stinkin' pitch count!"

OK, I lied. I never called Fergie—I don't even know him. I really did try to call him and had no luck. Do you know how many people named Ferguson Jenkins are in the phone book? None, that's how many! But if I had talked to Fergie, I'm sure he would have said something like, "Who the hell are you and how'd you get my damn phone number?"

I did however conduct an experiment designed to illustrate just how much pitchers are babied these days. I paid a kid in the neighborhood ten bucks to put on a catcher's mitt and catch me out at the local park. I measured off 60'6" and prepared to abuse my arm with an assortment of curve balls and my sizzling 46-mile-an-hour fastball. If I could throw, say 150 pitches or so, these young whippersnappers should certainly be able to do the same and more. Now keep in mind that I'm in my late fifties and the last time I pitched was about ten years ago with a whiffle ball in the backyard, so I was really taking a chance here. I could have caused some major damage to my arm.

Anyway, I stood there and fired away, breaking off curves and firing bee-bees. Every fifteen pitches, I would rest for about ten minutes as if I had completed an inning and my team was batting. I wanted to simulate real-game conditions as much as possible.

After having pitched three innings (45 pitches), I began to feel a twinge in my shoulder, but I continued on. After eighty pitches, my shoulder really began to ache and my elbow felt as if it was on fire, but I kept at it because I was determined to complete my experiment. On the eighty-sixth pitch I heard a loud pop in my elbow accompanied by a sharp pain and I had to stop. I could no longer lift my right arm above my waist without experiencing excruciating pain and I fell to the ground in tears. So, the neighbor kid ran home and got my wife who called me a stupid dumb-ass, grabbed a bag of ice, and drove me to the emergency room. I'm scheduled for Tommy John surgery in a couple of weeks.

You may be shaking your head and thinking I'm an idiot who failed miserably, but in truth I proved one important thing: Men in their fifties should be on pitch counts.

Chapter 31: It's Nothing Really, Just an Inflamed Achilles Elbow with Shin Splints

Remember Mark Prior? He was the guy all the experts said had—unlike oft-injured Kerry Wood—the perfect delivery. His "push-off and release" (baseball lingo for "push-off and release") were so perfect, Prior would never, ever be on the disabled list. In 2003, Prior won eighteen games and as 2004 approached, Cub fans were ready for even bigger things. He was our savior!

I like to keep a journal each year as the season unfolds so I can look back and see what was going on at various points and reminisce. Yeah sure, I'm a pathetic dork, but I don't golf, I don't hunt or fish, I don't belong to any clubs, and I'm not into coin or stamp collecting. Baseball and sex are my main interests and my wife pretty much controls the latter, so I tend to concentrate on the former.

*[Author's note: For those of you who really do think I am a pathetic dork, I assure you that I **do not**, repeat, **do not**, keep a journal. We are just pretending I do for the sake of this chapter. Just go along with it.]*

Anyway, I have taken some excerpts from my journal for the '04 season as they relate to the whole "Mark Prior Traveling Boo-Boo Show." I think from this little look back you will see that Prior's perfect "push-off and release" wasn't all that perfect. You will also see Cubs' doctors either sucked at evaluating the severity of injuries, or the Cubs organization was real good at lying to everyone. Either way, I was put on an emotional roller-coaster that nearly cost me my life.

February 21

Dear Diary,

Spring training is starting and I just can't wait to watch my Cubbies on their drive to a WORLD CHAMPIONSHIP! I just know Mark Prior is going to win, like thirty games, or something. I am so excited!

Think I'll go jogging and work off some of my excess energy.

March 1

Mark Prior is hurting a little bit—something to do with inflammation in his Achilles tendon. Wonder where that is??? He is expected to miss a few days of throwing. Nothing to worry about—just a little discomfort.

Time to go shoot some hoops.

March 2

Prior is being shut down for a couple of weeks just to be careful and make sure he is OK. It's just a minor setback. No biggie.

Think I'll go to the gym and work out.

March 7

Good news! Prior's Achilles is feeling better. No plans on when he will be ready to throw, but things are looking up. This is a happy day!

Gotta go to my Jazzercise class now.

March 11

Prior threw off flat ground in the bullpen today and said he felt good. Isn't that like just totally wonderful?

Time to do some lifting.

March 16

Mark threw off a mound today. Won't be long now. He should be ready by opening day! Goodie!

Now it's off to the gym to work on my pecs.

March 21

More good news! More throwing off the mound. He's gotta be getting close to being ready, don't you think?

Gotta go now. Heading to the Y to swim a few laps.

March 24

The Cubs announced Prior will start the year on the disabled list. Just a precautionary thing. Don't want to rush him back too soon and have him end up hurting his arm too. I think it's a smart move.

I was going to go work out, but I think I'm too tired.

March 25

Prior was supposed to throw in the bullpen today, but it was postponed. Something about a little discomfort. He'll try again tomorrow.

Screw the gym; I'm not in the mood.

March 26

This Prior crap is starting to get old. We are well into spring training now and he still has not thrown in a game. I don't see how he'll be ready to pitch in April. I'm starting to think they're messing with our minds.

Time to go to Dairy Queen for a couple of sundaes.

March 29

The Cubs are saying Prior is slowly coming along, but he will likely have to wait until May before he can start. This really sucks! I thought it was just a minor thing. What is going on???

I need a milk shake!

March 30

Doctors did a bunch of tests on Prior today and gave him a clean bill of health. That sounds pretty ominous to me. Every time they say he's OK, something comes up.

Think I'll go hang out with my friends at Mickey D's—maybe grab a couple of Big Macs.

March 31

See, I told you. Now it's his elbow and not his Achilles! What the hell?!! I mean which is it—his elbow or his Achilles? I'm no anatomy expert, but I think they're pretty far apart. Anyway, his elbow is hurting now, so it's going to be a while. May, my ass!

Man, a Dilly Bar sure would taste good now.

April 12

Prior continues to work out and throw pitches on the side, but he says he's still not ready to move up to the next level. I think the next level is T-ball or some crap like that.

Two Double Whoppers with cheese please!

April 24

It's late April and still no Prior. This is looking more and more serious. He's throwing on the side and he's feeling good (so they say), but it just seems like this is taking forever. It was only supposed to be a few days back in March. Then it was mid-April, and then mid-May, and this is really getting old. If his arm fell off, why don't they just say so instead of yanking our chains like this?

I'm depressed. I think a bucket of KFC will help.

May 5

Prior threw two innings in a simulated game today. Wow, that must have been really tiring. Better run some tests to make sure he didn't strain himself.

I wonder if Pizza Hut delivers at this hour?

May 7

Hey, here's good news: the Cubs moved Prior from the 15-day to the 60-day disabled list. Now that's progress!

I hear a hot fudge sundae calling my name.

May 18

The Cubs announced today that Prior will be going on a rehab assignment soon where he will be pitching underhand to an all-girls softball team in a simulated game. He will be on a 20-pitch count. Things are moving along well.

Cookies!

May 29

Prior is overpowering in his final rehab assignment against a little league all-star team. He is ready to go!

Think I'll do a sit-up.

June 3

The Cubs will activate Prior from the disabled list tomorrow. It's about friggin' time! He will be on an 85-pitch count when he makes his first start.

Two sit-ups!

June 4

Good news/bad news. Prior pitched today and looked great! Six innings, 2 hits, no runs, no walks, 8 Ks, 85 pitches. Of course, the bullpen blew it in the ninth and we lost 2-1. That sucks!

I'll walk up to DQ for a Brownie Earthquake.

July 15

Oh crap! Mark Prior just left the game in the second inning. Looks like it might be his Achilles again. I knew it—I just knew it! Things were just going too well.

Make that two Brownie Earthquakes!

Turns out it wasn't his Achilles, but rather his elbow again. Now they're saying he might not only miss his next start, but maybe the rest of the season. Now what are we going to do?

Yo quiero Taco Bell.

July 16

Good news! Tests show no ligament damage in Prior's elbow. They're even saying he might be able to start on Tuesday.

Think I'll do some jumping jacks!

July 20

Now they're saying he has "shin splints of the elbow!" What the fuck are shin splints of the elbow???! I think they're making this crap up! Anyway, he won't be pitching today. Not sure when he will pitch again.

Once more, I am depressed. Time for some DQ to get me back to my happy place.

July 30

Prior just isn't pitching well! It's not the same Mark we saw last year and I'm really worried that next they're going to tell us that he has "West Nile Virus of the patella" or some crap like that.

Wendy's...here I come!

August 21

He's still struggling—walking batters, hitting batters—it's just not the same Mark Prior.

I feel like sitting in a bathtub of hot fudge.

September 30

Good news! Prior's been pitching great again and he's starting to look like he did last year. Well at least we know we can count on him to pitch well in the playoffs!

I'd take a walk if I could get up out of this chair.

October 2

What playoffs? We finally have Prior throwing the ball well, and the rest of the team goes down the crapper!

Maybe an Arby's five-for-five deal will cheer me up.

October 3

This whole Mark Prior thing has really taken its toll on my physical well-being. I've gained 63 pounds this season just trying to deal with the emotional stress. My doctor says I'm going to have to find something less fattening than ice cream and fast food to get me back to my happy place.

He recommends drugs and alcohol...

Chapter 32: The Shot in the Mouth Heard 'Round Chicago

*I*f only Michael Barrett could have hit a ball as well as he could hit a face. Not that Barrett was a bad hitter of baseballs, but he never slugged a ball quite as well as he squared up A. J. Pierzynski's jaw.

Let's set our way-back machine to Saturday, May 20, 2006. A capacity crowd of Chicago baseball fans has filled U.S. Comiskey Cellular Park Field II to witness yet another fine interleague battle between my dear Cubbies and the despicable White Sox.

Sox catcher A. J. Pierzynski is an obnoxious turd to start with, but throw in the fact that his team is (it makes me sick to write this) the defending world champions (sorry for the puke stains) and you have a guy with the type of attitude that makes an otherwise mild-mannered Cub fan like myself want to smash him in the mouth. Of course I would never do that, what with the fact that he's about twenty years younger and roughly a foot taller than me and could probably crush my spleen with little effort.

Before we go further, you have to understand my mindset on this particular day. The White Sox are (do I really have to write these dreadful words again?) the defending world champions (I feel violated!) and have a 27-14 record. My Cubs, on the other hand, are the defending crap, mired in fifth place, and have won just four of their last twenty games including a 6-1 loss to the Sox on Friday. Because of these unfortunate facts, I have morphed into Howard Beale from the film *Network*: "I'm as mad as hell and I'm not going to take this anymore!"

Thankfully, Cubs catcher Michael Barrett knows exactly how I feel—maybe even more so. After all, he's had to crouch down behind the plate day-after-day as his team has suffered humiliation-after-humiliation. Plus he has to actually stand out on the field just a few feet away from the insufferable Pierzynski whenever one is standing in the batter's box and the other is in his crouch. It's a wonder Barrett hasn't cold-cocked the bastard already.

The game is scoreless in the second inning when Pierzynski tags up at third base on a fly ball to left field and comes barreling home after the catch. With absolutely no regard for Barrett's well-being or good sportsmanship, the big turd plows into the Cubs catcher who stands innocently waiting for the throw to home plate. The collision is audible throughout the ballpark as the two men come crashing to the ground. With the ball dislodged from Barrett's grasp, Pierzynski dramatically slaps his hand on the plate and then rises in victory. As he passes the stunned Barrett who is still gathering his bearings, the vicious animal violently shoulders him.

Now it's Howard Beale time. "That son-of-a-bitch!" I holler at the TV, phlegm spewing from my mouth. "Hit him! Hit that arrogant bastard!"

Barrett, as if hearing a voice from above, immediately obliges, hauling off and socking the big bully right in the jaw.

"Yes!" I shout as I leap up from my recliner. My beer goes flying across the room along with a bowl of Doritos. My wife is screaming at me—something about the new carpeting—but this is no time to worry about such minor concerns.

Both benches clear and a few players from both sides engage in actual fighting, while a majority of the players push and shove in typical "Eeew! I might break a fingernail or something" baseball-fight fashion. Eventually the umpires sort things out and eject Barrett as well as Pierzynski who triumphantly pumps his fists in the air and struts off the field like the jerk he is.

But who cares? What a high! I could almost feel my fist smashing into Pierzynski's jaw. I swear I could hear teeth rattle! It was awesome!!!

Inspired by Barrett's heroic poke, his teammates respond by allowing four more runs in the inning before ultimately losing the game 7-0. It will be just one of 96 losses we Cub fans would have to endure in 2006.

But that's not really important, because for one fleeting moment—through Barrett—I and millions of other frustrated Cub fans had the satisfaction of knowing what it's like to punch A. J. Pierzynski in the mouth, and holy crap t felt good!

So Michael Barrett, I thank you for that...

...and my spleen thanks you too.

Chapter 33: Retrospection Been Berry, Berry Bad to Sammy

*A*s if being a Cub fan isn't difficult enough, one of the things we've had to deal with over the past several years is reconciling our long love affair with a cheater. What adds to this mess is that those of us lucky enough to have been born with a brain (studies show that number at roughly 25 per cent of Americans) were aware that Sammy Sosa's amazing power surge from 1998 to 2004—along with that of many other major league hitters—couldn't have been completely legitimate. We saw it happening before our eyes yet we looked the other way too busy enjoying the sudden burst of moon shots to fully entertain the idea of what was igniting them.

Sammy's numbers were staggering: 66 home runs in '98; 63 more the following year; 64 in '01. And none of those totals were even enough to lead the league because other sluggers (cheaters) named Mark McGwire and Barry Bonds were topping the 70 mark. Something was definitely going on in baseball and excuses of smaller ballparks, lousier pitchers, and livelier baseballs weren't enough to explain it.

Sure we knew all along that Sammy wasn't just loading up on Flintstone vitamins, but it wasn't until all the fireworks had ended and Congress was conducting a 2005 investigation that we had to confront it. Not that we learned all that much from the congressional hearings— aside from the fact that McGwire doesn't live in the past, Roger Clemens is a prick (OK, we already knew that), and Sammy, conveniently, no habla Inglés.

Before the hearings, however, Cub fans did have to admit that Sammy wasn't above looking for any small advantage he could find. On the night of June 3, 2003, Sosa was caught using a "corked" bat in an interleague game against the Tampa Bay Devil Rays. Sammy broke his bat—shattered it, actually—and eagle-eyed umpire Tim McClelland discovered that the barrel-end of the bat was filled with cork. You wouldn't think that's such a big deal, but somewhere in the official rulebook of baseball is this silly thing about not putting cork in your bat, and blah, blah, blah. So, McClelland, using the authority vested in him by Commissioner Bud Selig and Major League Baseball, tossed Sosa from the game.

[Author's note: As a service to you, the reader, I looked up the official rule and its states, "You are not supposed to put cork in your bat, and blah, blah, blah..."]

After the game, Sammy—back in the good old days when English wasn't such a struggle for him—denied owning a corked game bat. He did admit to having a bat he used for batting practice that was filled with cork and he claimed he accidentally grabbed that bat by mistake. A reasonable mistake, right? Well apparently not, because according to some players, every hitter is intimately aware of every bat he owns. He knows the exact feel of every bat, and these naysayers insist that no major league hitter would ever mistakenly bring the wrong bat to the plate. I'm not a major league hitter, but I guess that makes sense. I don't think Eric Clapton would accidentally grab a banjo before he went on stage.

It really didn't matter how lame Sammy's explanation was anyway. We knew his bat was full of cork and he was full of shit, but we didn't care. Hell, we also knew his body was probably full of performance enhancing drugs, but we *still* didn't care. Just keep crankin' 'em onto Waveland, Sammy!

Crank 'em, he did, and love it, we did. Before each home game, Sammy would sprint to right field to the cheers of adoring fans who would rise in worship of their hero. We loved the little hop he did after smashing the ball into orbit. We didn't mind at all when he passed beloved icon Ernie Banks on the all-time Cubs home run list. We were mesmerized by his powerful blasts, his big personality, and his even bigger smile. We thought it was cute when, in his best Chico Escuela, he admitted that, "baseball been berry, berry good" to him. Sure, we knew he was a cheater, but in an era where every team had one, he was *our* cheater.

Yes Sammy was a cheater and we knew it, but we cheered his accomplishments anyway. We scrambled in the streets for his home run balls. We bought and wore his jerseys. We collected his baseball cards. And had the Cubs won a World Series with him in the lineup, we would have joyously celebrated. Sammy had become a god in Chicago and it wasn't only PDAs that made him so. Fans, the media, and Bud Selig looked the other way. We were all enablers.

But now, less than a decade later, the same fans who stood and cheered his prodigious clouts and bowed to the great Sammy Sosa despite knowing he was juiced, act as though he was the biggest villain to ever wear Cubbie blue. While jerseys with names like Sandberg, Grace, and Santo displayed on the backs are proudly worn at Wrigley Field, the Sosa jerseys are nowhere to be found. The 548 home runs, MVP award, and post-season appearances never happened.

Question a Cub fan how that could be. Ask a fan how he or she could have for years not only accepted Sammy's obvious flaunting of the rules, but cheered the results only to toss him aside when what had long been suspected had finally been confirmed. The fan will look uncomfortable and squirm like a witness at a congressional hearing before finally finding the right answer to your question.

"Uh... no habla Inglés."

Chapter 34: It Wasn't Supposed to End This Way

I had it all planned out. The Cubs were going to finally win the World Series and I was going to run naked through the streets, screaming and yelling and jumping for joy. But more importantly, the final chapter of my book was going to be all about how the Cubs had finally won it all! It would have been perfect—page after page of pain and frustration and anger and expletives followed by several pages of joy and elation and celebration.

But I've been around a long time and in all that time I've learned several things:

1. Nothing ever goes the way you plan

2. The Cubs are the Cubs

3. Running naked through the streets will get you arrested

There's just something about the Cubs that is unexplainable. Every time they come close, something crazy and heartbreaking happens. Goats, black cats, Gatorade and Bartman have all seemingly conspired to make life miserable for Cub fans. But why? Why can't we win it all just one time? Why not us?

For most of the past fifty years, the Cubs' lack of success was tolerable because the other Chicago baseball team hadn't won a World Series since 1917. The two teams were equally inept. Then the year 2005 came along and things got about as bad as they can get. It was a year from hell that ended with (this is the last fucking time I'm gonna write this!) the White Sox winning the World Series.

In 2007 the Cubs were good again and in '08 they had the best record in the National League and were favored to go to the World Series. But of course it was all just another big tease. That's what the Cubs do to you. They suck you in to the point that you start to believe success is right around the corner, and then you realize the corner is just a few thousand light-years past Pluto. And that's where we are right now. It is year one of the Theo era and I'm sure he'll turn things around and the Cubs will eventually be good again. And suddenly that corner will be a few feet away and we'll only be one out away from the World Series and then something crazy and disastrous will happen—something far worse than anything a goat or a Bartman could ever possibly do.

I can see it now. It's an easy fly ball to centerfield. Cub fans stand and roar in anticipation of the final out causing the entire ballpark to shake. The vibration is too much for the huge centerfield scoreboard as it rocks back and forth before crashing down onto the centerfielder killing him instantly. The ball falls safely to the ground allowing the tying and eventual winning runs to score. I throw a beer bottle at the TV, then bury my face in my hands and sob as my wife grabs the phone, hits the speed dial, and schedules yet another therapy session for me.

I know that sounds awfully pessimistic, but fifty years of watching improbable Cubs disasters have made me that way. But despite the fact that I am absolutely certain the Cubs won't ever get to the World Series until after I'm dead, I will continue to love them. I will continue to watch them. I will continue to hope that maybe, just maybe, our luck will turn. If you're a Cub fan—a true Cub fan—you understand why. You have to be a Cub fan to know what it is that keeps me coming back. I have been infected with something that has been with me since birth.

Because I really didn't have a choice—I was born to be a Cub fan. When you grow up in a family of Cub fans, you really have no choice. You can also be born with good sense, but it doesn't matter. The Cubs will still steal your heart, your mind, and your soul and you will spend the rest of your life with an incurable disease.

Photo Credits

Cover Photo

Photographer: Tina Kashmier

Director of Photography: Mary Jo Mucci

Wrigley Field Marquee

From the collection of Frank Mucci

Wrigley Field Rooftops

Photographer: Frank Mucci

APBA Cards

Photographer: Frank Mucci

www.ingramcontent.com/pod-product-compliance
Lightning Source LLC
LaVergne TN
LVHW051055080426
835508LV00019B/1884

* 9 7 8 0 6 1 5 8 7 5 1 2 5 *